*C*HERE LIES *C*OLORADO

FASCINATING FIGURES IN COLORADO HISTORY

By Richard E. Wood

Helena, Montana

ISBN 13: 978-1-56037-334-6
ISBN 10: 1-56037-334-2
© 2005 Farcountry Press
Text © 2005 Richard E. Wood
All gravesite photographs by Richard E. Wood unless otherwise noted.
Cover photo: background © 2005 JupiterImages Corporation;
       John Denver, Colorado Historical Society;
       Henry C. Brown, Colorado Historical Society, F4580;
       "Daddy" Bruce Randolph, African American Research Library,
       Hiawatha Davis Collection, and the Denver Public Library,
       Western History Collection, ARL229;
       Helen Bonfils, Denver Center of the Performing Arts;
       Emily Griffith, Denver Public Schools;
       Frank Eugene Amole, Jr., *Rocky Mountain News.*
Back cover photo: © 2005 JupiterImages Corporation.

For more information on our books, write
Farcountry Press, P.O. Box 5630, Helena,
MT 59604; call (800) 821-3874; or visit
www.farcountrypress.com.

Created, produced, and designed in the United States.
Printed in Canada.

09 08 07 06 05   1 2 3 4 5

Library of Congress Cataloging-in-Publication Data

Wood, Richard E.
Here lies Colorado / by Richard E. Wood.
   p. cm.
Includes index.
ISBN-13: 978-1-56037-334-6
1. Colorado—Biography. 2. Celebrities—Colorado—Biography. I. Title.
CT226.W66 2005
920.0788—dc22
2005017140

$\mathcal{D}$edicated to the memory of public safety professionals in Colorado who have lost their lives in the line of duty: from John Phillips, the first Denver police officer to be killed (1889), to Donald R. Young, who was killed in 2005.

May their memories and sacrifices be remembered always.

*T*ABLE OF CONTENTS

Era of Growth:
From Educators to Entrepreneurs

Modern Colorado:
"Rocky Mountain High" and To the Moon

ℱOREWORD

By Dick Kreck, *Denver Post* columnist and author
of *Murder at Brown Palace*

Pop-music singers are fond of crooning, "You're gonna miss me when I'm gone." Perhaps, but not for long.

One thing the dead can be sure of—while they can't take it with them, they're likely to leave something of themselves behind. Usually, it is photographs and personal letters (although in the age of e-mail, few of them will survive), bits of flotsam—and the memories of those who knew and loved them. But, after a generation or two passes and the deceased's memory begins to fade, what remains unchanged is an epitaph, etched in stone for a passing world as a signpost to their lives.

With *Here Lies Colorado*, Richard Wood focuses not on what his subjects said about themselves or what others said about them but on what they, in fact, left behind. It is not a book about those who have crossed into what authors called in long-ago days "the Great Divide." It is about their accomplishments, their legacies to Colorado and, in some cases, their foibles and follies, written with care and an understanding that they were not always well thought of in their day.

In the end—the one we're all destined to meet—*Here Lies Colorado* is about life, not death. Wood breathes life into those he chronicles, among them Henry C. Brown, whose hotel that bears his name remains central to Denver's social life; Governor Ralph Carr, who proved that humanity needn't end at the ballot box and can teach us a lot about tolerance in the face of public opinion; and

"Daddy Bruce" Randolph, a hard-working restaurant owner whose generosity captured a generation of like-minded citizens.

Some who were well known are barely recognized today, despite their accomplishments. How many, for example, recall Western novelist William MacLeod Raine, a best-selling author in the 1930s whose works rivaled in popularity that of Zane Gray? Or Barney Ford, an early-day black Denver businessman who overcame racial barriers to be a prominent hotel owner and restaurateur? Yet, their lives and deeds were no less relevant to their time than Horace Tabor or Charles Boettcher were to theirs. Some memorialized here, like cable pioneer Bill Daniels and photographer William Henry Jackson, are spending their eternal rest somewhere other than in Colorado. More's the pity.

In an increasingly crowded world, cremation is becoming more and more commonplace. But knowing that the few in this book sleep forever at Fairmount, Mount Olivet, or other cemeteries, peaceful places that are as much parks as they are burial grounds, tells us we can spend a few minutes visiting, and remembering them as they were.

When Wood and I first talked about my writing the foreword to this book, his only requirement was that I must include my own epitaph. What a daunting task! Who among us spends much time thinking of terrific last words that they would like to have the world gaze on? As a twenty-two-year-old, Benjamin Franklin did, in one of the most famous self-written epitaphs of all. Franklin, inventor, politician, diplomat, and, by many accounts, an all-around lover of life, chose the following for his headstone:

The Body of
B. Franklin, Printer
Like the Cover an old Book
Its Contents Torn out
And Stript of its Lettering & Gilding

Lies Here, Food for Worms
But the Work shall not be lost;
For it will (as he believ'd) Appear once More
In a New and More Elegant Edition
Revised and Corrected
By the Author

But when the time actually came for him sixty-two years later, he chose, perhaps gripped by second thoughts, a simpler tribute:

Benjamin and Deborah Franklin: 1790

Plain or simple, epitaphs are what they are and, with few exceptions, final. Some let their honoree's sense of humor shine through. Mel Blanc, the voice of dozens of Warner Brothers cartoon characters, lies beneath a stone at Hollywood (California) Memorial Park that reads, "That's All Folks!" Others may have had second thoughts, like mobster Al "Scarface" Capone, whose headstone reads, "My Jesus Mercy." But I suppose my favorite, oft quoted, is from author Robert Fulghum, who recalled that his dying friend, in a moment of whimsy, chose, "If only I could get through this week."

When I wrote *Murder at the Brown Palace: A True Story of Seduction & Betrayal* and discovered that the beautiful young woman in the scandalous 1911 double murder at Denver's luxury hotel lay buried in New Jersey without a headstone, I arranged with the publisher to have a gray granite stone placed at her grave. But what to put on it? Except for what I read, and wrote, about the woman, I didn't know her. After several discussions, we decided to go with her name, birth and death dates, and her nickname, "Sassy," which epitomized her life and, hopefully, her personality. The irony was, of course, that eighty-five years after her death, men were still buying her gifts.

All of which does nothing to help me pin down the parting words to be, literally, etched in stone. But, barring having my ashes tossed overboard at the Golden Gate Bridge in San Francisco, I believe it would read, "Thanks for having me. Can we do it again?" Make of that what you will, passing world.

As for the rest of them, read 'em and weep.

$\mathcal{I}$NTRODUCTION

By Richard E. Wood

*"The grave itself is but a covered bridge
leading from light to light, through a brief
darkness."*

—Henry Wadsworth Longfellow

For some, a gravesite—if it exists—is relatively unimportant; this was particularly true on the Western frontier. As John Wayne said in *The Cowboys,* one of his last movies, "It's not how you're buried, it's how they remember ya." Yet most people seem to have a desire to place physical markers or memorials as remembrances of loved ones—and leave markers behind themselves. Even John Wayne wanted a headstone, albeit a small and modest one. He did not get his wish, incidentally, and is now buried in Newport Beach, California, under a bronze plaque that depicts Wayne on horseback in a Western scene.

In many Western towns, formally platted and carefully tended public cemeteries didn't come into existence until late in the community's development. Until then, burials might take place at churchyards or family plots. But for most people, relatively anonymous burials were common, as were interments in unpleasant, unsanitary, and unattractive areas on the outskirts of town marked off as a "graveyard" or "Boot Hill."

The idea of formal and attractive parklike cemeteries began in this country in the early nineteenth century in places such as

Philadelphia and Boston, where the Mount Auburn Cemetery, built in 1831, bills itself as "American's first garden cemetery" and is a national historic landmark. Gradually, the idea of cemeteries as parks began to take hold in the West, and such places even began to be regarded as a sign of a community's maturity and civilization.

For many people, the choice and design of a final resting place for themselves or for the recently deceased is a way to establish and memorialize a legacy. Georges Clemenceau, French Prime Minister in the early twentieth century, died in 1929—with the memory of German aggression in the Franco-Prussian War of 1870–71 and the bloody "Great War" of 1914–18 still fresh in his mind. A widely circulated, although probably apocryphal, story about Clemenceau is that he was buried in a specially designed grave in which he was placed standing up, facing Germany, as a symbol of the need for vigilance. President John F. Kennedy's "eternal flame" gravesite at Arlington National Cemetery has become a national shrine to his memory. Napoleon's Tomb, at Les Invalides in Paris, is one of the city's most popular landmarks, as is Lenin's Mausoleum in Moscow. In each case, the gravesites have become a focal point of the person's historical legacy. And Grant's Tomb in New York City was immortalized for several generations by Groucho Marx, who offered losing contestants on his television quiz show a consolation prize if they could tell him "Who was buried in Grant's tomb?"

Most of the people who made Colorado what it is today are memorialized by a physical marker, or at least a location, marking their life and passing. Many are still remembered and honored by later generations of their family or friends. Visit a cemetery and you will usually find visitors tidying up, placing flowers, or perhaps bringing a small folding chair and just sitting in the sun beside their friends or loved ones. Thinking, remembering, smiling, weeping.

You may also find people like Gail Meyer Kilgore, a member of the Colorado Tombstone Transcription Project. The goal of these "digital graveyard" projects, which have counterparts throughout the world, is to catalog and photograph every tombstone and structure—especially those that are crumbling or in disrepair—and preserve them for posterity. There is also a trend toward "interactive" gravesites, with tombstones that play video or audio of and about the deceased. And the ubiquitous internet has entered the picture, with "virtual gravesites" and blogs, featuring online memorials to loved ones.

The idea to create this book, another symbol to memorialize the deceased, is not an original thought. Books have been written about noteworthy citizens of certain communities, from military heroes to celebrities. It was after reading a similar book about my own birthplace of Kansas City that I began to wonder what became of some of those Coloradoans whose names are still with us today: the Speer of Speer Boulevard, the King of King Soopers, the Gart of Gart Sports, as well as others whose names may be less well known but who also played their role in the development of The Centennial State.

The result of that curiosity is *Here Lies Colorado*. Some of the people in this book were famous, some notorious. Others were obscure and are virtually forgotten. In this book, their lives and contributions can be remembered, their stories allowed to live again.

Selecting people to profile in this book was a distinct challenge. Some choices were easy, including Aspen's "odd couple," John Denver and Hunter Thompson. Colorado became a center stage of 1970s popular culture thanks to Thompson's best-sellers and the songs of John Denver who, it has been observed, was to the music of the 1970s as the Beatles were to the 60s, Elvis to the 50s, and Sinatra to the 40s.

But other choices were more difficult. For example, why include sporting goods entrepreneur Jerry Gart and not printing entrepreneur A. B. Hirschfeld? Why journalist and activist Eugene Cervi and not *Denver Post* editor Palmer Hoyt? Ultimately, space and format limitations forced difficult choices to be made. However, future volumes of this book are contemplated, and I hope readers will participate by suggesting names of people they believe would be of interest to general audiences. Also, I welcome information that may correct any mistakes that have occurred or may add specifics that will improve any future editions.

A word about the organization of the book. Here, too, difficult choices had to be made, as some people and their families spanned more than one era. I have tried to place the person in the era during which his or her greatest contribution was made or, in the case of families, where the contribution of the oldest member of the family was made.

As I visited cemeteries to research *Here Lies Colorado,* I realized what should have been obvious: these places are at least as much for the living as for the dead, just as funerals help meet the needs of the survivors in addition to providing a ceremony for the deceased. I hope this book will inspire readers to make an effort to learn more about their own ancestors and, if possible, to visit the gravesites of friends and family, and to take advantage of the unique attractions of cemeteries, from the parklike spaces of Denver's Fairmount to the small cemeteries and the many unrehabilitated graveyards throughout Colorado and the west.

The analogy in the quotation by Longfellow that began this introduction seems to me an apt one. Although Longfellow saw the grave as a bridge to the afterlife, a grave also can serve as a symbolic bridge from past generations to present ones, and from our history to our future.

$\mathscr{H}$ENRY CORDES BROWN
1820–1906

Henry Cordes Brown was forty in 1860 when he and his second wife, Jane, came through Denver, then just a small mining camp on the banks of Cherry Creek. He was on his way to California from Ohio, where he had been a successful carpenter and builder. The idea to stay appears to have originated with Jane, although accounts vary on her motivation. Some say she fell in love with the beauty of the area. Others believe that she feared Indian attack and refused to go farther. In any event they stayed, and Brown turned from carpentry to real estate development.

He built a small house at Eleventh Avenue and Sherman Street on Brown's Bluff, now Capitol Hill, where he acquired 160 acres. The cost of the land was reportedly $200. He also bought an unusual triangular piece of land at Seventeenth Street and Broadway, which he used as pasture for some cattle. As he developed the 160-acre parcel, he made a major contribution to the city by insisting that streets on his property be laid out in a conventional north–south grid, rather than the skewed diagonal design of the streets in downtown Denver, which followed the line of Cherry Creek.

To stimulate interest in Brown's Bluff, in 1868 he donated ten acres to the territory of Colorado for a capitol, and he and many of his friends built mansions along Grant and Sherman Streets. An economic panic in 1877 caused Brown to sell his house to Horace Tabor, who was in the process of moving to Denver after having made his fortune in Leadville. By the 1880s Brown had more than recovered

Henry C. Brown.
COURTESY OF THE COLORADO HISTORICAL SOCIETY, F4580.

his fortune. He was active in the founding of the Denver Tramway Company and the Board of Trade, and land sales on Capitol Hill went well as the area became fashionable.

Whether the prospect of rising land values made him regret his donation to the state or whether he was, as he insisted, simply irked by the state's failure to build a capitol building as quickly as he had hoped, Brown sued in 1879 to recover the property. The case dragged on until 1886, when the United States Supreme Court ruled against him. The state finally began construction, but Brown refused to attend the 1890 dedication.

By that time, Brown's attention had turned in another direction: toward that triangular piece of land downtown, the project for which he would remain famous to this day.

Denver was growing fast, and Brown decided that it needed a better hotel. There is a story that Brown had a falling out with the owners of what was then Denver's best hotel, the Windsor, where— as the story goes—Brown was once refused admittance because he was wearing cowboy clothing. Whatever his motivation, Brown hired Frank Edbrooke, perhaps Denver's most famous architect, to design what he hoped would be Denver's finest hotel.

The project began in 1888 at Seventeenth Street and Broadway, using Colorado red granite and Arizona sandstone for the Italian Renaissance exterior. But it was the interior that caught the imagination of the public. Edbrooke designed the first atrium hotel lobby in the United States, rimmed with elaborate cast iron railings, and topped by a glass ceiling. Also, because of the triangular shape, the building was designed so that every room faced outward, with views of either the mountains or the plains. By the time of its completion, the hotel had cost more than $2 million, a huge amount for that day, and at nine stories, it was also the tallest building in Denver.

A long-standing urban legend is that a tunnel was constructed under Tremont Street from the Brown Palace to the Navarre building across the street, where gambling and prostitution were available. According to the legend, men staying at the hotel could be transported by small rail cars through the tunnel to the Navarre without being observed. Although the remains of what appeared to have been tracks were reportedly found in the Navarre's basement, there is no proof that the tunnel actually existed, let alone that it was used in the manner suggested by the legend.

Although the Brown Palace has been open every day since business began on August 12, 1892, it got off to an inauspicious start. Less than a year after the opening, Colorado was hit by the silver panic of 1893, followed by a depression and the collapse of many Denver banks. Creditors were at Brown's doorstep as attempts were made to sell or foreclose on the hotel. The ownership of the property was confused for many years, being sought—and claimed—by several of Brown's associates, including David Moffat, Maxcy Tabor, William Bush, and W. S. Stratton.

In 1894 Brown, who was by then a seventy-four-year-old widower, raised eyebrows by his marriage to nineteen-year-old Mary Mathews. By 1900 the couple were divorced, and Brown, who was tiring of the struggle to keep the hotel, retired to California, where he died in 1906. The battles over management and ownership of the hotel continued until the 1920s, when it was sold to Horace Bennett and Charles Boettcher.

Despite the problems, Brown's reputation remained intact. People were fond of the hotel he had built, and remembered him for his charitable impulses, which included funding for the first public library in Colorado. Although he died in California, his body was returned to Colorado for a public viewing. It was held, ironically, in the rotunda of the state capitol, which had been the focal point of his bitter six-year legal battle with the state, and he was buried at Fairmount Cemetery.

More than a century after Brown's death the 241-room hotel he created remains one of Denver's most popular attractions and a national historic landmark. The rich and the famous have made "the Brown" their home while in Denver, including Winston Churchill, most U.S. Presidents beginning with Theodore Roosevelt in 1905, and scores of entertainment stars, from The Beatles to Bono. President Eisenhower made the Brown Palace virtually a western White House and spent many summers in an apartment on the hotel's top floor with his wife, who was a Denver native.

Gravesite of Henry C. Brown.

Colonel John Chivington in his army
uniform in Denver, early 1860s.
COURTESY OF THE DENVER PUBLIC LIBRARY,
WESTERN HISTORY COLLECTION, Z128.

ℐOHN MILTON CHIVINGTON
1821–1894

John Chivington's place in history is defined by the two military actions he led. The first, in 1862, made him a Colorado hero with a bright political future. The other, just two years later, ended his career and destroyed his reputation.

The early years of Chivington's life offered few clues as to his destiny. He was born in Ohio, and by the time he was twenty-three he had married and was running a business. In 1844 he became a Methodist minister, moving to Missouri in the 1850s, where there was considerable secessionist and pro-slavery sentiment. But Chivington was an outspoken opponent of slavery, and eventually some parishioners threatened him with violence. The next Sunday the six-foot-four-inch, 260-pound Chivington defiantly ascended the pulpit with a Bible in one hand and a revolver in the other and was soon dubbed "the Fighting Parson."

Perhaps tiring of the controversy, Chivington decided to move west, reaching the friendlier political climate of Denver in 1860, the same year South Carolina seceded from the Union.

With the firing on Fort Sumter in 1861, the Civil War began. Offered an option to join the Union forces as a chaplain or a soldier, Chivington opted for the latter—becoming a major with the First Colorado Volunteers.

By 1861 the Confederates were making progress on all fronts, and troops from Texas had invaded New Mexico Territory and claimed it for the South, with its capital at Mesilla. The discovery of gold in Colorado attracted the attention of the Confederates, who planned to seize the mines and perhaps claim the rest of the Colorado Territory as well. The threat was real.

By February 1862, Confederate troops had captured Albuquerque and Santa Fe and were poised to invade Colorado. The Colorado Volunteers were sent south and encountered the Confederates in the Sangre de Cristo Mountains near Santa Fe. On March 26, Chivington attacked with his advance unit of about 400 men, driving the enemy back. The two sides then battled inconclusively for the next two days until March 28 and the Battle of Glorieta Pass, during which Chivington's troops were able to strike a decisive blow when they destroyed the Confederates' supply camp at Canoncita. For the Union, the Battle of Glorieta Pass was a much-needed victory—ending any serious Confederate threat in the West, and occurring when Union troops elsewhere were on the defensive. Nationally, the tide of battle would not turn decisively against the South until July of 1863.

Back in Colorado, Chivington, now a Colonel, was a hero—the man who saved the state from rebel forces. His name was mentioned as a rising star in political circles.

As the threat of Confederate troops receded, concern about Indians increased. The tribes that had been on the eastern slope of Colorado—primarily Arapaho and Cheyenne—had been pushed from one area to another as treaties were broken repeatedly. They were relegated to remote and barren places, far from the buffalo herds on which they depended.

Although there had been sporadic Indian violence, unprovoked attacks were rare. Nevertheless, many settlers favored policies ranging from expulsion of the Indians to outright extermination. Chivington leaned toward the latter option, which was also strongly endorsed by the *Rocky Mountain News* and its editor, William Byers. Chivington had rescued the Byers family from the flood of 1864, and the two men, along with Territorial Governor John Evans, were friends and allies.

Any hope of a peaceful solution to the "Indian problem" was dashed in June of 1864 when, for unknown reasons, four Arapahos attacked a ranch near Denver, brutally murdering a rancher, his wife, and their two daughters. What remained of the mutilated victims' bodies was displayed in Denver. The headlines of the *News* screamed for revenge, and the population was scared.

Governor Evans turned to the hero of Glorieta Pass. Chivington, eager to take care of the Indians once and for all, headed after the culprits, but the Arapahos could not be found. After several months, Chivington was frustrated. Finally, on the morning of November 29, 1864, he came upon a group of Cheyennes, led by Chief Black Kettle, near Sand Creek in southeastern Colorado. In fact, the tribe was living at a spot marked by an American flag Black Kettle had been given, and where he had been told they could camp in safety.

Chivington ordered an attack on the unsuspecting Cheyennes,

John Chivington's tombstone at Fairmount Cemetery.

and before the dust had settled some 160 Indians had been killed—mostly women and children. The incident touched off a wave of Indian unrest that would continue for five more years.

Chivington returned to Denver triumphantly, proclaiming his victory at the "Battle of Sand Creek." But in the days that followed, an ugly story began to emerge from some of his own troops. It had been, they said, a massacre.

A government investigation followed and confirmed the allegations. It had indeed been a massacre, perhaps the worst atrocity in the country's history. Evans was removed as territorial governor and Chivington left the army in disgrace, although he faced no criminal charges. Black Kettle and the Cheyenne were pushed out of Colorado and into Oklahoma. There, just two days short of the fourth anniversary of Sand Creek, Black Kettle was killed during an attack led by Colonel George Custer. It was later to be called the Washita Massacre.

In 1865 Chivington left Colorado, and eventually ended up back in Ohio. An effort to re-enter politics there in the 1880s ended when his role in the Sand Creek Massacre was revealed, and he returned to Colorado, where he still had many admirers and where he worked as a deputy sheriff in Denver until his death in 1894. He is buried at Fairmount Cemetery.

In 2000 the Sand Creek Massacre National Historic Site was created, and two years later a ranch on the site was given to the Arapaho and Cheyenne tribes as permanent trust lands. In addition, a plaque characterizing Sand Creek as a "massacre" rather than a "battle" was unveiled at the veterans' monument at the Colorado State Capitol—a monument that previously had honored, among others, the government officials and soldiers responsible for Sand Creek.

$\mathcal{B}$ARNEY L. FORD
1822–1902

Barney Ford was one of many people who came to Colorado in its territorial years, one of the few who earned wealth and success, and the only one of this elite who had started life as a slave.

Ford's story is a remarkable one. Starting as a slave in Virginia, his life followed a path of accomplishment over a period of eighty years: from a plantation to a riverboat, then escape via the Underground Railroad to Chicago, south to Nicaragua, then to Denver and Breckenridge, Colorado, and Cheyenne, Wyoming. All the while he was building successful businesses, raising a family, and wielding significant political influence.

The roots of Ford's success went back to his childhood and his mother, Phoebe. She instilled in him strong desires for education and freedom: to learn to read and write, to speak well,

And—eventually—to escape from a life of slavery.

In the years before Ford was able to make his way to the North, he worked as a slave, cooking on small steamboats in the south. In 1846 opportunity presented itself when he was sold to the captain of the *Magnolia Blossom*, a large paddlewheeler on the Mississippi River. Unlike the earlier boats, the Magnolia plied waters that bordered on states that offered the prospect of freedom.

With the help of a white friend on the *Magnolia*, Ford—dressed as a woman—made his escape in Illinois. He eventually made his way to Chicago aided by the loose organization known as the

Barney Ford.
COURTESY OF THE COLORADO HISTORICAL SOCIETY, F6323, F25835.

Underground Railroad, a clandestine network of people who helped thousands of slaves escape from the South.

In Chicago, Ford married Julia Lyoni, began helping the Underground Railroad, and became a successful barber. In 1848 gold had been discovered in California, and by 1851 the Fords had saved enough money to sail for the West, via Central America, to get their share of the gold bonanza.

They made it as far as Nicaragua. While waiting for a passage to California, Barney Ford began to have second thoughts. He encountered many passengers returning from California and learned that the search for gold was far more difficult than he had believed. Ford also saw an opportunity: catering to the travelers going through the area. During the next few years Ford opened and managed two successful hotels in Nicaragua, although eventually the volatile political situation, brought about by a civil war in Nicaragua, became too much for him. In 1856 he sold his businesses and returned to Chicago.

In 1860 Ford arrived in Denver, again following the lure of gold, which had been discovered in Colorado in 1858. Although Ford filed claims on land in the foothills and in Breckenridge, he lost one claim to white claim jumpers and the rest to a crooked lawyer. Ford again turned to barbering and opened shop in Denver, later adding a small restaurant. He began to take an active role in politics, particularly civil-rights issues, and worked with William Hardin and other leaders in Colorado's small black community to oppose efforts to admit Colorado to the Union without guaranteeing minorities the right to vote.

Ford's businesses were so successful that a local banker offered to back his expansion, and his People's Restaurant at 1514 Blake Street, with a bar and a barbershop, became even more lucrative. The menu featured what would become a Ford trademark: fresh oysters, no small trick when travel to the nearest ocean took a week or more.

Ford continued to work for civil rights and went to Washington several times to lobby on different issues, including the effort to protect minority rights in territories such as Colorado. In Colorado he fought against segregated schools and was the first black to run for elected office, an unsuccessful try for the Colorado House of Representatives. In that election, Ford's image as a wealthy Republican businessman and a political power broker led opposition Democrats to label him the "Black Baron of Colorado," a nickname that stuck.

By the 1870s Ford and his wife had opened successful hotels and restaurants in Denver, Cheyenne, and Breckenridge—establishments that hosted the era's most prominent travelers, including

Barney Ford's tombstone at
Riverside Cemetery.

Colorado's Early Years: Opportunity and Open Spaces

President Grant at Ford's Inter-Ocean Hotel in Cheyenne. From an unlikely beginning, Ford had become a leading member of the Denver business community, a board member of a local bank, and a pillar of the Republican Party, with a large house in the fashionable Capitol Hill neighborhood. Eventually, Ford was able to make up for his unsuccessful gold mining efforts. In the 1880s he became a partner in a successful Breckenridge mine, and his investment was said to have returned over 3,000 percent.

The 1890s were years of slowing down for Ford, whose wife died in 1899. The economic depression of 1893 hit Ford hard, but because he had little debt, he managed to live relatively well in his retirement thanks to income from his real estate. Ford died on December 14, 1902, and is buried at Denver's Riverside Cemetery.

Ford's remarkable story has been told in several books and articles. He is remembered as well by Barney Ford Elementary School in Denver, a historical marker on Blake Street, and Barney Ford Hill—site of an old Ford mining claim and now part of the ski area in Breckenridge. And he finally made it to the Colorado legislature. Not as an elected official—one of his few unfulfilled goals—but in a commemorative stained glass window that overlooks the House chamber.

Horace Tabor in the 1880s after his marriage to "Baby Doe" and his term in the Senate.
FIELD COLLECTION. COURTESY OF THE DENVER PUBLIC LIBRARY, WESTERN HISTORY COLLECTION, X22028.

"Baby Doe" Tabor in her twenties as the new Mrs. Horace Tabor.
FRED MAZZULLA COLLECTION. COURTESY OF THE DENVER PUBLIC LIBRARY, WESTERN HISTORY COLLECTION, X22030.

Maxcy Tabor in a studio portrait circa 1890.
ROSE AND HOPKINS PHOTO. COURTESY OF THE DENVER PUBLIC LIBRARY, WESTERN HISTORY COLLECTION, H-93.

Augusta Tabor in the 1870s.
COURTESY OF THE DENVER PUBLIC LIBRARY, WESTERN HISTORY COLLECTION, X21985.

*H*ORACE AUSTIN WARNER TABOR
1830–1899

*E*LIZABETH McCOURT
"*BABY DOE*" TABOR
1862–1935

*A*UGUSTA PIERCE TABOR
1833–1895

*N*ATHANIAL MAXCY TABOR
1857–1929

Only one opera, *The Ballad of Baby Doe*, and only one Broadway musical, *The Unsinkable Molly Brown,* have been written about Coloradans. They both feature people who spent significant portions of their lives in Leadville, a coincidence that may seem strange today because Leadville is a small, struggling town that clings to Colorado's fading history as a mining center. Yet, Leadville was once a thriving community with a population more than ten times that of today, and with great wealth—in the form of minerals—pouring out of the mountains surrounding the town, which sits at 10,430 feet in elevation.

The Unsinkable Molly Brown, a lighthearted musical, was the second most successful work by Meredith Willson (after *The Music Man*) and told the story of Margaret Tobin (Mollie) Brown. In contrast, the tragic *Ballad of Baby Doe* opera tells the sad story of Elizabeth McCourt (Baby Doe) Tabor, second wife of Horace Austin Warner Tabor, "The Silver King."

Horace Tabor was born in Vermont in 1830. He became a stonecutter, married Augusta Pierce in Maine in 1857, and they moved west to a farm in Kansas. By 1860, with their young son Maxcy, they headed to Colorado, attracted by stories of mining strikes in the mountains west of Denver.

Finding gold proved to be more difficult than expected, and the Tabors turned instead to running small mercantile stores, primarily in Lake County and ultimately in Leadville, one of the largest and most prominent mining towns in the state. Horace Tabor was active in Leadville politics and held several offices, including postmaster and mayor. He avoided mining himself, although he occasionally speculated by buying shares in others' mines. In the spring of 1878 he offered to provide a couple of miners with the provisions they needed—perhaps worth $50 to $100—in return for a one-third interest in a mine they planned to dig near Leadville. It was an arrangement known as a "grubstake," the kind of transaction Tabor had done frequently, if unsuccessfully, in the past.

1878 was different, and Tabor's life changed dramatically. His "partners" struck it rich at the mine, known as the Little Pittsburg. The mine turned out to be extremely lucrative, producing as much as $10,000 in silver in a single day. Tabor's return on his small investment soon amounted to hundreds of thousands of dollars. His luck continued, with similar successes at mines like the Chrysolite and the Matchless, and by 1879 the Tabors were among the wealthiest people in Colorado, with a fortune worth more than $100 million in today's money. Tabor became famous and began promoting Colorado mining investment opportunities in the east. Many mining company securities were traded on stock exchanges in New York and London, where they soared to unrealistic heights in a frenzy of speculation, only to collapse in the early 1880s—after Tabor and his associates, including David Moffat and Jerome Chaffee, had sold most of their investments.

Never looking back, Tabor began to diversify, buying bank stocks and building ornate opera houses in Leadville and Denver, where he also built the city's first "skyscraper" (five stories high) at Sixteenth and Larimer Streets and bought a mansion near Seventeenth Street and Broadway. His political life blossomed, too, and he was lieutenant governor and briefly served in Congress in 1883, filling out the term of Senator Henry M. Teller who had been appointed Secretary of the Interior. He might well have been elected to a full Senate term of his own had it not been for his private life.

By the time of the strike at the Little Pittsburg mine in 1878, his relationship with Augusta—a practical and serious woman who disliked his easy-going ways and penchant for speculation—had become strained. Adding to the difficulties, Tabor had begun seeing other women, including some residents of the thriving red light districts in Leadville and Denver.

Meanwhile, in 1879 a young couple from Wisconsin arrived in the Colorado mountains. Harvey Doe and his attractive, baby-faced wife, Elizabeth, began mining in the area around Central City. When their marriage fell apart in 1880, Elizabeth moved to Leadville. She was eighteen years old, and had already acquired the nickname "Baby" Doe. She attracted the attention of most of the men in Leadville, including the fifty-year-old millionaire playboy, Horace "Silver Dollar" Tabor, who soon gave up his other female companions for her.

Tabor's relationship with Doe became public knowledge when he moved her to Denver, and in 1883 Augusta finally and reluctantly consented to her husband's requests for a divorce. That same year Tabor married Baby Doe in Washington, during his brief tenure in the Senate. Most of the women of Washington society stayed away from the wedding to protest Tabor's scandalous behavior. After the Tabors moved back to Denver and were living in an elaborate mansion near Thirteenth Avenue and Sherman, most Denver "society women" did likewise. The Tabor–Doe story continued to be a favorite subject of gossip for years thereafter, spiced by the news that before his Denver divorce from Augusta in 1883, he had obtained a questionable ex-parte "divorce" in Durango in March of 1882 and had entered into a secret, and possibly bigamous, marriage to Doe in St. Louis in September, 1882.

Nevertheless, Horace and Doe Tabor and their two children, Elizabeth Bonduel Lillie and Rosemary Silver Dollar Echo, lived happily and well for the next ten years and contributed a great deal to the growth of both Denver and Leadville. Tabor's political career had been derailed because of his private life, but his investments enabled him to afford a luxurious lifestyle, even though some of the mines were beginning to be depleted, and unsuccessful speculations were forcing him to borrow more than usual.

Then, swiftly, it all came to an end. In 1893 the silver market collapsed in the severe depression of that year. To make matters worse, that same year Congress repealed the Sherman Silver Purchase Act of 1890, which had provided artificial support for silver prices. The over-extended Tabors were ruined. Unable to maintain the mansion, they moved to a much smaller house.

Tabor tried his best to pay off his debts and even returned to the mountains to begin prospecting again. In 1898 Tabor's political friends were able to secure his appointment as Denver postmaster— a popular choice as Tabor, sixty-eight, had by then assumed the status of a pioneering elder. In the spring of 1899, however, he became ill with a then-inoperable case of appendicitis. Baby Doe and the children returned from a trip to New York, and they and his son Maxcy were with him when he died, peacefully and happily, on April 10, 1899. Reportedly, his last word of advice to his wife referred to one of the mines that had been his most productive: "Hold on to the Matchless Mine." He received a respectful, elaborate, and well-attended state funeral and was buried at a since-abandoned Catholic cemetery on Capitol Hill.

Although tempted to return to New York, Baby Doe, thirty-eight, decided to stay in Colorado, and after a short time in Denver

The gravesite of Horace and Elizabeth "Baby Doe" Tabor at Mount Olivet Cemetery.

Augusta Tabor's grave at Riverside Cemetery in Denver.

Maxcy Tabor is buried at the Babcock family gravesite at Fairmount Cemetery.

she went back to the much-reduced town of Leadville. Her daughters soon left, but for the next thirty-five years she stayed on in a dilapidated cabin near the played-out Matchless Mine, dreaming unrealistically of ways to recover the lost Tabor fortune. Her body was discovered on March 7, 1935, frozen to death in her cabin. She was returned to Denver for burial at Mount Olivet Cemetery, and Horace Tabor's body was moved to be beside her.

As for Augusta, she apparently remained deeply in love with Horace Tabor and was hurt that he never returned to her. Financially, however, she may have been fortunate. After her divorce she received a large settlement, which she managed well. She lived quietly and respectably, well-liked by the people of both Denver and Leadville. The financial difficulties of 1893 bothered her very little, and soon thereafter she moved to California, where she died in 1895. Her son, Maxcy, brought her body back to Denver and buried her at Riverside Cemetery.

Maxcy lived until 1929. At the time of his death Maxcy, who had arrived in Denver in 1859 when he was nearly two years old, claimed to be the last surviving member of the '59-ers—the pioneer group made up of those who had arrived in Denver before 1860. Maxcy's career followed the path his father had set. He worked for several years as treasurer of the Tabor Opera House, although his relationship with his father was strained, probably because Maxcy had tended to side with his mother during the acrimonious divorce proceedings. He also worked for a time with the Brown Palace ownership group, and tried various other businesses, including mining. Unlike his father he never struck it rich, although an article in the *Leadville Herald* after his death describing him as "almost penniless" may have overstated the case. He lived modestly at 1120 Grant Street with his wife, Lou Babcock Tabor. It was at the Grant Street house that he died on January 21, 1929, at the age of seventy-one. He is buried with his wife at the Babcock plot at Fairmount Cemetery.

The story of the rise and fall of the Tabors has intrigued people for more than a century. In 1956, Douglas Stuart Moore's opera *The Ballad of Baby Doe* premiered at the Central City Opera House. Two years later it opened in New York, with Beverly Sills in the role of Baby Doe, and many books and articles have been written about the Tabor saga.

"Baby Doe" Tabor in 1930 at the age of sixty-eight, spotted on a visit to Denver.
COURTESY OF THE DENVER PUBLIC LIBRARY, WESTERN HISTORY COLLECTION, Z232.

William N. Byers.
COURTESY OF THE *ROCKY MOUNTAIN NEWS.*

The Byers family gravesite at Fairmount
Cemetery.

$\mathcal{W}$ILLIAM NEWTON BYERS
1831–1903

Denver's first newspaper—hitting the streets on April 23, 1859—was the *Rocky Mountain News*, founded by twenty-eight-year-old William Newton Byers, who had arrived in the small settlement on the banks of Cherry Creek just six days earlier. Byers ran the *News* until 1878; those nineteen years saw Denver growing rapidly and Colorado gaining statehood. Byers and his newspaper were instrumental in both developments.

Byers was born in 1831 in Madison County, Ohio, but by the 1850s his family had moved to Iowa, and soon thereafter Byers moved to Omaha, Nebraska, where he worked as a surveyor and was a member of the city council. When stories of gold strikes in Colorado reached Omaha in 1859, he saw an opportunity to move West and start a newspaper. Although he had done some writing, including a diary of a trip along the Oregon Trail, he had no formal background in journalism. Nevertheless, he bought a printing press from a defunct Nebraska newspaper, loaded it on a wagon, and in March 1859, he headed for the Rockies—a trip of forty-two days through heavy spring snows.

Most of the stories that had reached the East created the impression that there was more going on in Denver than was in fact the case. When Byers arrived, he found little more than a few mining camps in the area. The new towns of Auraria and Denver had been established only six months earlier and numbered no more than a thousand permanent residents between them.

Undaunted, Byers set up his press in a rickety wooden building above a saloon and began publishing in April 1859, just minutes ahead of the rival *Cherry Creek Pioneer*. Displaying some ingenuity, Byers had written most of the copy for his first edition while he was still in Nebraska. All that was needed was to insert a fresh story on the front page and the *Rocky Mountain News* was in business. Byers was able to do this because much of the content of the paper consisted of little more than highly imaginative articles extolling the wonders of the new territory, as yet unseen by Byers. For example, Byers predicted a great future for Denver as a port, a reference to its location on the often ankle-deep Platte River, which he portrayed as a navigable waterway. Another time, in an effort to convince railroads that they easily could build lines west from Denver, he dismissed the Rocky Mountains as being just a little "hilly."

Frontier journalism was a tough business. After Byers published stories attacking the lawlessness of a gang of thugs that patronized the Criterion Saloon at Fifteenth and Larimer—today Larimer Square—they retaliated by raiding the *News* office and kidnapping Byers. The Criterion's owner persuaded them to let him go, but soon after he returned to the office, the thugs came back, shooting to kill. Byers and his employees returned the fire, mortally wounding one of the attackers. Thereafter, rifles became standard office equipment at the *News*.

Byers was an avid outdoorsman, and much of his spare time was spent exploring the West, particularly hiking, camping, and climbing in the Colorado mountains. In 1864 he began traveling to the area that is now Estes Park, visiting often with Joel Estes and his family, and Byers generally is credited with having named the area after Estes. Following several unsuccessful attempts, Byers climbed Longs Peak in 1868, the first recorded ascent of the 14,255-foot peak, although certainly the Arapaho Indians had done so long before. Both Byers Peak and the Byers Peak Wilderness Area in the Arapaho and Routt National Forests are named after him.

As the owner of the first and most successful newspaper in Denver, Byers became part of a powerful group of local leaders. It soon became clear that for Byers, the newspaper was but one tool in the greater cause of attracting settlers to Denver—and coincidentally displacing the Indians who had lived in the area for centuries. Another tool was politics. Byers had been involved in Republican Party politics in Nebraska, and he stayed involved in Colorado. Appointed by President Abraham Lincoln, Byers served as postmaster from 1864 to 1867.

Two other local leaders with whom Byers became acquainted were Colonel John Chivington, head of the Colorado militia, and John Evans, the territorial governor. The three would soon figure in one of the most notorious episodes in Colorado's history.

In June 1864, in a rare attack, Arapaho Indians committed the grisly murder of a young cowboy, his wife, and their two daughters at a ranch near Denver. Hysteria swept the white settlers, fanned by lurid headlines in the *News* and Byers's call for "a few months of active extermination against the red devils." In August, Governor Evans ordered Colonel Chivington into action. Three months later, his troops had failed to locate those responsible for the murders; but on the morning of November 29 they launched an unprovoked attack on some Cheyenne Indians camped near Sand Creek in southeastern Colorado, killing 160—primarily women and children.

The initial response to the attack was favorable—particularly in the pages of the *News*. However, as details of the attack became known, opinion began to change. What had originally been called "The Battle of Sand Creek" became "The Massacre at Sand Creek." Following an official investigation, Chivington lost his command and was forced out of the army. Evans and Byers remained unrepentant and were never heard to regret their part in the tragedy. Apparently the sacrifice of innocent Cheyennes in the cause of assuring Easterners that the West was "safe" was a satisfactory result for Byers and Evans.

In the late 1860s the railroads decided the "hilly" land west of Denver was impractical for rail traffic and built their major east–west line through Wyoming. Byers and his associates, including David Moffat, whose dream of a rail passage through the Colorado Rockies would eventually be his undoing, were devastated. They feared the decision could turn Denver into a ghost town. However, a burst of financing and activity followed, with the result that by 1870 Denver had a connection to the east–west line in Wyoming, and was also the terminus of a line linking Denver directly to Midwest rail hubs. The burgeoning metropolis was saved.

Byers appeared to many to be a logical choice for governor or senator of the new state of Colorado, but his political career came to an abrupt end in 1876 when the public learned that Byers, a married man, had been having an affair with a divorced woman. The affair burst into the news when the woman tried to kill him after he informed her that he had no intention of divorcing his wife, Elizabeth. The scandal proved fatal to his chances for political office.

Byers sold the *News* in 1878 but remained prominent in Denver for the rest of his life. He helped start the Colorado Historical Society and the Chamber of Commerce, and in the 1880s was a founder of the Denver Tramway Company.

Byers died in 1903 at the age of seventy-two and is buried at Fairmount Cemetery. His wife, Elizabeth, who had stayed with him despite the affair, lived until 1920 and remained active in the Society of Colorado Pioneers—a group that she and her husband had helped create to honor those who came to Colorado before 1861.

The Byers–Evans house at 1310 Bannock Street in downtown Denver still stands as a museum. It was built in 1883 by Byers and sold in 1889 to William Evans, a business partner of Byers, and the son of Byers old friend, Governor John Evans.

$\mathcal{J}$OHN WESLEY ILIFF
1831–1878

To most Coloradans, the name Iliff is associated with a school of theology and a street in Denver. Yet, in the mid-nineteenth century, John Wesley Iliff, was "the cattle king" and was largely responsible for developing cattle ranching into what eventually would become one of Colorado's most important businesses.

Iliff was born in Ohio, where his father was a successful farmer and rancher. He attended Ohio Wesleyan College and began working for his father, who offered to stake him to a farm of his own in Ohio. However, when Iliff heard about opportunities in the West, he persuaded his father to give him $500—a substantial sum in those days—and in 1857 he headed to Kansas. Two years later, hearing stories about mining discoveries further west, Iliff moved on to Colorado Springs and Denver, where, like fellow pioneer Charles Boettcher, he made his living not in mining itself, but in selling supplies to miners from a store near the banks of Cherry Creek.

According to some accounts, Iliff became interested in the ranching business after seeing the great demand for beef at his store and knowing how difficult it was to meet that demand. Whatever the motivation, in 1861 he took advantage of his background and entered the ranching business near Fort Morgan, eventually acquiring thousands of acres, much of it adjoining the Platte River, and stretching north into Wyoming.

Ranching today is a challenging business, but in the old West it was even more difficult. In addition to the problems faced by all

John Wesley Iliff.
COURTESY OF THE DENVER PUBLIC LIBRARY,
WESTERN HISTORY COLLECTION, F4694.

Iliff family statue and graves, including John
Iliff's wife Elizabeth and Elizabeth's second
husband Reverend Henry White Warren,
whose grave is just to the right of the statue.

entrepreneurs, ranchers in Colorado in those days had to deal with Indian unrest and uprisings, severe water shortages, rustlers, inadequate transportation systems, land-use fights with farmers, and the economic uncertainties of a frontier economy.

Iliff was not a stereotypical cattle baron—at least as that kind of character has been portrayed in movies and television. He abstained from alcohol or tobacco, seldom carried a weapon, and was soft-spoken. He also had a strong religious background. He had been named after John Wesley, founder of the Methodist Church, and he often expressed an interest in starting a school in Colorado where ministers could be trained.

In 1865 Iliff was married to Sarah Smith, but within a year of the marriage she died following the birth of their son. However, Iliff's business prospered. He was awarded contracts to supply beef to the labor forces building railroads in the West, and also to supply army forts. Once the railroads were operating, Iliff's ranches shipped thousands of head of cattle to Midwest packinghouses. So extensive were Iliff's holdings that it was said he could travel from one end of his property to the other for a full week before having to spend a night on land he didn't own. At its peak, the Iliff ranching business owned more than 25,000 head of cattle and spread out over more than 10,000 acres.

In 1870, Iliff was married again—this time to Elizabeth Fraser, from Fitzroy, Ontario. They lived briefly in Cheyenne, where Iliff had started a bank. Frontier Cheyenne didn't appeal to Elizabeth, however, and in 1873 they moved to Denver. Elizabeth was uncomfortable with Wyoming's "progressive" equal-rights agenda and, according to the family, she didn't like the idea of exercising the newly won rights of women to sit on juries because to do so would require her to mingle with "her social inferiors." John and Elizabeth had three children and lived at Eighteenth and Curtis Streets. In 1878, Iliff—who was just forty-seven—became ill with an obstructed gall bladder.

He died on February 9, 1878. Initially, he was buried at Riverside Cemetery, but in 1920 his body was moved to a family plot at Fairmount.

If the Iliff story had ended with his death, he would be known today just for his cattle and land businesses. After his death, Elizabeth remained in Denver, managing his businesses and raising the children. In 1883 she married Methodist Bishop Henry White Warren. Remembering her late husband's oft-expressed interest in creating a school to train ministers, Elizabeth was determined to honor his memory. She played a central role in both the religious and educational development of Denver, including, in 1884, making a founding contribution to what would become the Iliff School of Theology. Initially, the school was linked to the financially troubled University of Denver, and Elizabeth and Henry Warren feared that the university—to which they were also major contributors—might try to use theology school funds to prop up its own finances. The theology school was closed from 1900 to 1910 while Elizabeth worked, successfully, to separate it from the University of Denver.

Today, the Iliff School of Theology is a Methodist seminary, although students represent many different religions and denominations. Although Iliff continues as an independent institution from the University of Denver, the schools cooperate, and Iliff students have access to many of the facilities at the university and to several joint-degree programs

In 1889, the Warrens built Fitzroy Place, named after Elizabeth's birthplace, at South Cook and East Warren Streets in Denver, where they lived for most of the rest of their lives. Elizabeth Iliff Warren died on February 14, 1920, and she and her second husband are buried in the John Iliff plot at Fairmount Cemetery.

CHIEF OURAY
1833–1880
CHIPETA
1843–1924

The enduring interest in Ute Indian Chief Ouray is justified by his complex personality, his impact on the events that transformed Colorado and wrote the final chapter in the story of the fragile existence of Indian people as independent "nations," and—not least—by the overriding tragedy of his life and times.

As is the case with much of Indian history, the story of Ouray is shrouded in a past that is indistinct and was documented primarily by white writers. Although he is commonly regarded as "Chief of the Utes," in fact the Utes were a disparate and nomadic people with many small tribes and many chiefs. Ouray, who was born near Taos, was not even a full-blooded Ute. His father was an Apache and he was raised as a Spanish-speaking Catholic in a heavily Spanish community. As a teenager, Ouray lived a relatively privileged life with a Spanish family after his parents moved to western Colorado to join a Ute tribe.

Ouray received a surprisingly good education for his time and circumstances and grew up able to speak Spanish, Ute, Apache, and some English. He also became accustomed to the relatively cosmopolitan life of northern New Mexico and the Santa Fe Trail, where he came into contact with traders and travelers who spoke many languages and represented many cultures. In contrast, as pointed out by P. David Smith in his 1987 book *Ouray, Chief of the Utes,* most of the

Chief Ouray and his wife **Chipeta** in a
formal portrait in 1880, the year he died.

Utes living in Colorado in the 1830s and 1840s had never even seen a white man.

Ouray had also learned something else as a result of his life in a strategic part of New Mexico: the United States was a very formidable military power. He had seen the U.S. Army quickly dominate all opposition during the Mexican-American War in 1846 and put down a Pueblo uprising in 1847. He was impressed with the size and equipment of the troops, particularly in contrast to the small and relatively ill-equipped forces that the Indian tribes could muster.

In 1850 Ouray left New Mexico to join his father, who by that time had become a chief in a Ute tribe in southwestern Colorado. Ouray belatedly began to adopt the Ute culture and traditions as his own, and in 1853 he was married to Black Mare, who was probably a Ute. In 1857 his only child, a son, was born and his wife died. Life for Ouray consisted primarily of hunting and fishing, interspersed with forays into combat against other tribes, where he earned a reputation as a very skilled fighter. He also became one of the chiefs in the tribe.

During the 1850s and 1860s several Indian tribes, including Southern Ute tribes, raided white settlers. Retaliation by the U.S. Army was swift and overpowering, which was no surprise to Ouray based on what he had seen earlier in New Mexico. He came to a sad, if realistic, conclusion: the whites were not going to go away and it would be futile to stand in their path. This realization influenced his actions for the remaining years of his life.

As Ouray began to emerge as a Ute leader he was faced with two choices. He could use his skills and intelligence as a warrior to resist the white encroachment and see his fellow tribesmen perish or be banished to reservations, or he could try to use diplomacy and tact to delay as long as possible the onrushing white tide, and to preserve as much as possible of the Ute people and their culture.

Ouray's approach was generally consistent with that of his fellow Utes, who had a reputation among whites as a trustworthy and peaceful people. During his two decades of leadership, however, there were some, including other Ute chiefs, who were frustrated by the policy of accommodation and what they saw as Ouray's overly compliant nature.

Two years after the death of his first wife, Ouray married Chipeta, a full-blooded Apache girl of sixteen who had been raised by the Utes; they found her after her parents died in a raid by a tribe that was an enemy of the Apaches. Although many Utes practiced polygamy, and Ute marriages were often relatively informal, Ouray and Chipeta made a lasting and faithful bond and were well-suited to one another. They remained virtually inseparable until his death and shared a common yearning for peaceful coexistence with whites rather than war. After his marriage Ouray assumed greater responsibilities as a chief and was effective in dealing with white emissaries, including Kit Carson. Carson was an Indian agent in New Mexico and he became a good friend of Ouray's—and was sympathetic to the Indian cause.

By 1862 Ouray had become the leading negotiator for the Utes, at least in the eyes of the whites, who had difficulty understanding the nature of the Ute's decentralized and seemingly informal tribal government. For convenience they tended to lump all the Utes together into one group with Ouray as its leader. In fact, Ouray led only the Tabeguache (or Uncompahgre) tribe. The other Ute tribes were scattered and not in agreement about who could speak for them and what concessions they were prepared to make to the white settlers.

In 1862 Ouray met and negotiated with the Colorado territorial governor, and in 1863 he was a member of a Ute delegation that traveled to Washington and met with President Lincoln. Later that year the first of several treaties was signed between the federal government and the Utes, which in theory gave the Utes most of Colorado west of the Continental Divide, and also promised them money, livestock, and other benefits. The government benefits failed to materialize in the quantities promised. Settlers continued to move onto lands that had been reserved for the Utes, and several of the Ute tribes did not recognize the 1863 treaty.

As Ouray was assuming tenuous leadership of the Utes, he suffered a personal tragedy in 1863 when his five-year-old son was kidnapped by a band of Sioux during a raid on a Ute hunting camp on the Front Range. Reportedly, the Sioux later traded the boy to an Arapaho tribe. Ten years later, Ouray's lost child would be a pawn in negotiations between the government and the Utes.

By 1868 it was clear that the 1863 treaty was ineffective, and Ouray and other Utes again went to Washington for negotiations, resulting in a new treaty that pushed the Ute border west from the Continental Divide but still promised them most of western Colorado and a smaller area in Utah. Again, the government also agreed to provide support for the Utes, in the form of money and livestock, along with two Indian agencies, schools, farming tools, and seeds.

Although the treaty indicated that white settlers would be kept out of the Ute territory—and promised the land to the Utes "forever"—little effort was made to prevent whites from entering the area, let alone to remove existing settlers. In 1871, when gold was discovered in the San Juan Mountains within Ute territory, whites poured into the region unmolested. The government decided it needed more Ute territory, particularly the land on which mining discoveries were being made. Ouray realized then, if he hadn't understood it earlier, that the treaties were not worth the paper on which they were written. But he had no attractive options. Some in the tribe wanted to fight, and there were plots against Ouray when it was discovered he was willing to negotiate again with the government. While Ouray shared his opponents' mistrust of the whites, he believed that armed resistance meant suicide.

In an effort to entice the Utes back to the bargaining table, Felix Brunot, the head of the Board of Indian Commissioners, initiated a manhunt for Chief Ouray's kidnapped son. The hunt eventually produced a teenage boy who was never conclusively identified as Ouray's son and who, in any event, chose to remain with the Arapaho tribe with which he was living rather than go with Ouray and the Utes. Although he was disappointed by the outcome, Ouray was impressed by the effort the government had made and also by the government's promise of land and a pension. Even as whites were streaming into the disputed San Juan mining area and achieving de facto control, Ouray and a majority of the Utes agreed to cede the land to the government in the Brunot Treaty of 1873. Although their empire was steadily shrinking, the five or six thousand Utes still owned—at least on paper—much of western Colorado and part of Utah.

The ink was not long dry on that paper, however, before white settlers began edging outward from the San Juan mining areas into Ute land. Ouray and Chipeta moved into a well-furnished home on a farm near Montrose, provided at government expense as an inducement for them to demonstrate an example of the kind of farming and ranching life the government wanted the Utes to adopt. Ouray, whose health had begun to weaken as a result of a serious kidney ailment, and Chipeta, who seemed to enjoy farming, accepted their new lifestyle. But many Utes did not welcome the effort by the government to restrict their traditional hunting forays outside their territory, and they found it difficult to accept the more settled agricultural lifestyle being promoted by the government.

An uneasy peace followed the 1873 treaty, with constant minor violations on both sides. Neither Utes nor whites were really happy with the treaty. Many Utes longed for a return to their more nomadic heritage, and many whites really wanted the Utes to be expelled from Colorado altogether and moved to reservations in Oklahoma or to Utah. The situation simmered for six years until it boiled over in the events that led to the Battle at Milk Creek, and The Meeker Massacre.

The stage was set for the tragedy in 1878 when Nathan Meeker was appointed Indian agent for the Utes, who were divided between a "peace" faction headed by Ouray and a "war" faction headed by Ute Jack. Meeker, sixty-one, had been a newspaper reporter and was a protégé of *New York Tribune* publisher Horace Greeley. He became a founder of the utopian Union Colony in Greeley, Colorado, in 1870, where he started a newspaper. Whatever skills he had as a reporter did not carry over into publishing, and by 1878 he was deeply in debt and somehow managed to be appointed an Indian agent at the White River Agency in northwestern Colorado—a position about which he had neither knowledge nor training. He showed little sensitivity to the issues or people he was dealing with and was determined to force the Utes to adopt his strict and idealistic views of what constituted civilization.

In September 1879 following a dry summer that left many of the Utes hungry, violence broke out at the White River Agency when Meeker ordered a Ute race track plowed up. Horseracing was a traditional Ute custom, but Meeker opposed it. He disapproved on moral grounds of the gambling that went with it and felt the Indians were wasting supplies feeding racing horses rather than farm animals. A brief fistfight between Meeker and one of the Indian sub-chiefs led him to send for reinforcements. The cavalry, under the command of Major T. T. Thornburgh headed from Wyoming toward Ute territory. The Utes regarded Thornburgh's arrival as an invasion, and both the Ute leaders and Meeker himself urged Thornburgh to halt while he was still a day's ride from the agency. Stubbornly, Thornburgh chose to proceed and rode into a well-laid Ute ambush, in which he, his officers, and many of his troops were killed. Shortly thereafter, on September 30, the Utes turned on the whites at the agency, killing Meeker and eleven other men and holding the women for ransom.

After a week, General Wesley Merritt and 300 troopers arrived to relieve the remnants of Thornburgh's cavalry and re-take the agency where the Indians, at the request of Ouray and other chiefs, already had agreed to cease fighting. Ouray also helped lead the effort to obtain the recovery of the white women, who eventually were taken to his home where they were cared for and released.

Although responsibility for the Milk Creek and Meeker incidents was shared by both sides, it was the Indians who would pay the greatest price. The incidents provided all that was necessary to convince the government that the Utes' tenuous ownership of much of western Colorado had to end. An 1880 treaty effectively moved most Utes to a desolate, arid reservation in northeastern Utah, leaving only a very small reservation in southwestern Colorado near Mesa Verde. Although Ouray's health was failing rapidly, he once again traveled to Washington, where his stature was such that he was able to meet with both President Rutherford B. Hayes and Secretary of the Interior Carl Shurz to defend the Utes who had attacked the cavalry and to argue—to no avail—against removing Utes from Colorado. He pointed out the provocations of Meeker, and while he did not excuse the actions of those who had participated in the massacre at the agency, he did argue that they should receive a fair trial in a neutral venue. By then, most of the Utes who had taken part in the massacre had fled the area and were never heard from again.

Ouray's health continued to deteriorate after his return to Colorado and he died on August 24, 1880, at the Southern Ute Agency near Ignacio. He was forty-seven. Ouray's body was buried in a secret ceremony at a cave nearby.

The treaty of 1880 was finally ratified by the Utes, but only after intense lobbying and some controversial cash payments by Otto Mears, a successful entrepreneur in the San Juan Mountains area who built toll roads and railroads into mining areas. Mears had a vested interest in making sure the 1880 treaty took effect and the Utes were removed from the area.

A year after Ouray's death, most Utes left Colorado—the land they had called home since before the birth of Christ—for their new

The official Colorado memorial to Chief Ouray and Chipeta is located at the Ute Indian Museum and Ouray Memorial Park in Montrose, Colorado. Chipeta's grave is nearby on the park grounds, and Chief Ouray is buried near Ignacio, Colorado.

home on a reservation in Utah. Chipeta, by then increasingly disillusioned and resentful, was forced to give up her bountiful farm and attractive home in Colorado for a small, poorly furnished house in Utah. She remained on the reservation—often living in a teepee—until 1924, when she died at the age of eighty-one near the appropriately named Bitter Creek. In 1925 there was an effort to have the bodies of both Ouray and Chipeta moved to Montrose for reburial on their farm. Chipeta's body was reinterred in what is now the Ouray Memorial Park near the Ute Indian Museum. Ouray remained near Ignacio until his body was exumed and reburied at the local cemetery in a large ceremony.

Ouray and Chipeta remain controversial to some who are critical of their accommodative policy toward whites. Yet it is difficult to imagine any better outcome for the Utes, or the other tribes living in the path of U.S. westward expansion and settlement, and it is easy to imagine worse outcomes, such as befell tribes such as the Pequots, Yamasees, and Powhatans in the East, and the Chiricahua Apache and other Plains Indians in the west who had pursued a policy of war and resistance. Chief Ouray managed to keep the Ute people intact, and enabled them to bargain on more equal terms with the government than were accorded most other tribes.

Compared to many other tribes of the 1800s, the Utes today have a strong culture and a relatively good life and promising future. Portions of the desolate land that they were given by the government have turned out to contain bountiful natural gas reserves, which have provided economic support for members of the tribe.

In the end, Ouray was playing a delaying game with the few and inadequate resources he had and probably made the most out of an impossible situation.

$\mathcal{D}$AVID HALLIDAY MOFFAT
1839–1911

The man sometimes called "the Cecil Rhodes of the Rockies" or "the Empire Builder," David Halliday Moffat may have saved the small town of Denver from oblivion when it was bypassed by the railroad in the 1860s.

Moffat was born in Washingtonville, New York, on July 22, 1839. At the age of twelve he struck out on his own for New York City, where he became a bank messenger and soon rose to the position of assistant teller. In 1855 he joined an older brother in Nebraska, where he sold real estate, although he had to do business through older intermediaries since he was just seventeen at the time and was too young to enter into contracts. He moved on to Denver in 1860, opening a successful retail business, Moffat's Book and Stationery Store. In 1862 he married his childhood sweetheart, Fannie Buckhout of Saratoga, New York, and became one of Denver's first successful entrepreneurs, living in the finest downtown residential area at Eleventh and Larimer Streets. He returned to banking in 1866 as a cashier at the First National Bank and became the bank's president in 1880. He later moved to 1706 Lincoln Street and, just before he died, he built an elaborate mansion at Eighth Avenue and Grant.

In 1867, after failing to persuade the Union Pacific to include Denver in its east–west rail system, he joined with Walter Cheesman, former territorial governor John Evans, and others to found the Denver Pacific Railway. The Denver Pacific competed suc-

David Moffat at his desk in 1900.

cessfully with the Colorado Central and in June 1870 became the first link between Denver and major east–west railroads. The Denver Pacific railroad, and the extension to Denver of the Kansas Pacific railroad from Kansas City in August of 1870, saved Denver from being bypassed by the most important transportation network of the day, and in all likelihood saved Denver from being reduced to an inconsequential small town, existing in the shadow of Cheyenne. Moffat also built narrow-gauge railroads to Leadville and other mining towns. He stayed active in railroading until the end of his life and served for many years as president of the Denver & Rio Grande.

In the 1870s water was becoming a growth industry. Denver's increasing population made it difficult to rely on wells, and people had long since abandoned getting their water directly from the rivers and streams they shared with livestock and dogs.

Moffat partnered with William Byers to start the Denver Artesian Water Company in 1870, but their well was unproductive. Even deep wells couldn't keep up with demand, and it became clear to Moffat that Denver would have to look elsewhere for water. He joined with Cheesman and James Archer to found the Denver City Water Company. In 1872 they began pumping, first from Cherry Creek near the Platte River, later moving south to a plant at Twelfth Avenue and Shoshone, which received its water via ditch directly from the Platte. The Denver City Water Company was productive, but the quality of the water was a problem. In 1879, forty people died as a result of a major typhoid epidemic, and Denver finally began to work on developing a modern water and sewer system.

Moffat also invested in several mining ventures, including the Caribou Mine near Nederland and Horace Tabor's Little Pittsburg bonanza in Leadville. He sold most of his mining interests in the early 1880s, before the collapse of the industry. Controversy surrounds the ethics of Moffat's market timing in disposing of his mining stocks, with some charging use of insider information, others just chalking it up to his skills as a shrewd businessman.

In 1889 Moffat and Chessman started Citizens Water Company. Their concerns about water quality led them farther south on the Platte. For two years, competing water companies engaged in "wars," using such weapons as price-cutting and sabotage. By 1894 Moffat's company prevailed, acquiring its competitors and forming the Denver Union Water Company, which received an exclusive franchise to supply water to Denver. The company was bought by the city in 1918 and became the Denver Water Board.

As the nineteenth century came to an end, Moffat was nearing sixty. His First National Bank, which had weathered the panic of 1893, was a dominant Denver institution—in part, some say, because at the height of the panic, Moffat very publicly deposited a large amount of cash in the bank in an effort to demonstrate its safety. Personally, Moffat also had survived an 1889 robbery, when he was confronted at gunpoint in his office by Tom McCarty, a confederate of Butch Cassidy. McCarty got away with $21,000 and, after pulling a few more robberies, disappeared.

In 1900 Moffat turned his attention to the enormous challenge of building a year-round rail line to the West through Colorado over the Continental Divide. Construction of the Denver, Northwestern & Pacific, which began in 1902, proved to be a nightmare, plagued by high costs, weather problems, and the opposition of competitors. By 1911 the "Moffat Road," as it was called, almost had exhausted the substantial resources of Moffat, his bank, and many investors. Moffat went East in his ornate private railway car, "The Marcia," named after his daughter, to try to raise money to keep his dream afloat, but was turned down. On March 18, 1911, he was found dead in his room at New York's Hotel Belmont. There was speculation that he may have taken his own life, although the general conclusion was that he had died as a result of the shock of not receiving the investment he hoped for—and the prospect of imminent bankruptcy.

His wife moved out of their mansion at Eighth and Grant, and back to 1706 Lincoln, where she stayed on in a few rooms as a renter. Moffat was buried inconspicuously at Fairmount Cemetery. It would not be until 1921 that the *Denver Post* launched a campaign to rehabilitate Moffat's reputation and properly mark his grave. The legislature created Moffat County out of Routt County. Craig, the Moffat County seat, marked the farthest point the Moffat Road reached in its quest for Salt Lake and the Pacific before its collapse. Moffat's restored private Pullman car, "The Marcia," which is in the Craig City Park, is one of the county's most popular and important historical monuments.

Moffat is remembered primarily for the historic 6.4-mile tunnel under the Continental Divide that bears his name. Finally completed in 1927 by the Moffat Tunnel Commission, a public agency, it cut the distance between Denver and the Pacific by 176 miles and is still being used by the Union Pacific, Amtrak, and the Denver Water Board, successors to the railroad and water companies started by Moffat over a hundred years ago.

David Moffat's gravesite at Fairmount Cemetery.

Thomas M. Patterson in 1902.
COURTESY OF THE COLORADO HISTORICAL SOCIETY, F8392.

$\mathcal{T}$HOMAS MACDONALD PATTERSON
1839–1916

For the better part of forty-five years, Thomas MacDonald Patterson, politician and publisher, greatly influenced the development of Colorado—including helping to create a viable two-party political system, and running a daily newspaper that championed many unpopular causes.

Patterson was born in Carlow County, Ireland on November 4, 1839. His family immigrated to New York City in 1849, and four years later moved to Indiana, where Patterson worked in newspaper offices while going to high school.

When the Civil War started, Patterson enlisted on the Union side but also found time to continue his education at local colleges and to marry Katherine Grafton in 1864. After the war, which claimed the life of his brother, he studied for the bar in New York, and became a lawyer in 1867. In 1872 he moved to Denver, where he got involved in politics, became city attorney, and served as a member of the Democratic National Committee from 1874 to 1880. While Colorado was still a territory, Patterson was elected as a delegate to Congress, where he was instrumental in obtaining statehood for Colorado. In 1876 he became the state's first member of Congress—an election in which Patterson was the only Democrat to win a major office. Even so, his victory was so close and controversial that the issue had to be settled by the House of Representatives. Defeated for re-election in 1878, he returned to Denver and resumed his career as a successful trial lawyer. He also handled many cases that—in later years—would be considered civil-liberties cases, involving unpopular causes or minority clients.

In 1888, Patterson, who was by then living at Seventeenth and Welton Streets, returned to electoral politics, unsuccessfully facing another lawyer, Republican Job Cooper, in that year's gubernatorial election. In 1890 Patterson bought a controlling interest in the *Rocky Mountain News*, and as publisher of the paper he was deeply involved in many of the issues in Colorado during the turbulent 1890s and early 1900s. The state suffered greatly during the depression and financial panic of 1893 and endured a political crisis in 1894 when Governor Davis Waite of Aspen—Colorado's only Populist gover-nor—called out the militia to march on Denver's City Hall to remove what many believed were corrupt local officials.

The political atmosphere was volatile. Anti-Waite forces mobi-lized behind the American Protective Association (APA), which took advantage of the economic depression to promote a "jobs for Protestants" agenda at the expense of Catholics and others. In 1895 Waite was replaced by Albert W. McIntyre, who had received the APA's endorsement and was governor until 1897. The *Rocky Mountain News* played a key role in successfully countering the APA's destruc-tive influence, leading the way for the election as governor of Patterson's fellow Democrat, Alva Adams.

The 1904 gubernatorial election gave Patterson another opportunity to use the pages of the *News* to take on powerful opponents—in this case the Colorado Supreme Court. The out-come of the gubernatorial election was controversial. Democrat Adams appeared to have won re-election, but his election was overturned by the legislature in a controversy over court appoint-ments. Patterson, accusing the court of dishonesty and of being politically motivated, was found guilty of contempt of court. However, public opinion was in his favor after he eloquently chal-lenged the court's verdict and offered to provide proof of his allegations. He received only a minor censure from the court, but gained public approval.

In 1900 Patterson had returned to politics and served one term in the United States Senate after defeating Democrat Charles S. Thomas, a former governor and also his former law partner. By this time Patterson had become active in the Populist Party, and he was elected to the Senate on a fusion ticket of Populists, Republicans, and Democrats, united primarily by their economic and silver policy. It was the beginning of an informal coalition that, depending on the issues, linked Patterson with people such as Judge Ben Lindsey, who worked to improve the juvenile court system, civic-reformer Ed Costigan, and others. The political machine of Mayor Robert Speer—one of the Democrats who had worked for Thomas in the senatorial race—was a frequent target of this coalition.

Patterson gravesite at Fairmount Cemetery.

The early years of the twentieth century saw the beginnings of one of the country's longest lasting newspaper wars. The *News* had been in business since 1859 and had long been Denver's most successful paper, while the *Denver Post* began its existence in 1892 as a weekly paper. This changed in 1895 when the *Post* was bought by Harry Tammen and Frederick Bonfils. Relying on a formula of promotions, editorial crusading, and sensationalism, the Post began to take circulation away from the *News*. After a brief "cease-fire" in the newspaper war, when the Post actually endorsed Patterson for the senate, the battle resumed, with the *News* often using its columns to attack the *Post's* publishers, Tammen and Bonfils, as proponents of "yellow journalism." The war came to a head in 1907 when Patterson was physically attacked by Bonfils one morning while walking to work. Bonfils had taken exception to having been characterized in the pages of the *News* as a "blackmailer." The confrontation was recorded for posterity in *Timberline,* Gene Fowler's colorful story about the *Post's* owners. The sixty-seven-year-old Patterson charged that the forty-seven-year-old Bonfils had—to use Fowler's word—given him two "wallops" to the head. A court agreed, and Bonfils was fined fifty dollars and warned to leave Patterson alone.

Patterson sought political office one more time. In 1913, at the age of seventy-four, he sold the *News* and began his last campaign: a three-way race for governor. Progressive candidate Ed Costigan split the Democrat/Progressive vote with Patterson, and Republican George Carlson was easily elected. Patterson died on July 23, 1916, at the age of seventy-six, and is buried at Fairmount Cemetery in a family plot with his wife Katherine, who had died in 1902.

$\mathcal{F}$RANK E. EDBROOKE
1840–1921

The physical transformation of Denver from a ramshackle Western mining town, with buildings that were little more than shacks and false fronts, into something resembling a true city was due in large part to the efforts of Colorado architects such as Frank Edbrooke.

Edbrooke was born in Chicago in 1840 to a family of builders and architects. After serving in the Civil War and then working in his family's business in Chicago, he headed west as an architect for the Union Pacific Railroad. He came to Denver in 1879—barely twenty years after the mining camp of Denver had sprung up on the banks of Cherry Creek and the Platte River. Denver's population was less than 35,000, and Colorado had been a state for just three years.

The thirty-nine-year-old Edbrooke came to Denver to help in the design and construction of two of the city's first real urban structures: the Tabor Grand Opera House at Sixteenth and Curtis Streets, and the Tabor Block, a commercial building at Sixteenth and Larimer Streets that has since been replaced by the Tabor Center, a shopping and entertainment mall. Horace Tabor, the Leadville mining millionaire, contracted with Edbrooke and his brother, Willoughby, for the two projects. Both buildings have been demolished, but they served to put Denver on the map, architecturally. The style of the Opera House would be followed by Edbrooke himself and other architects in the design of many subsequent Denver buildings, including Denver's first great hotel, the Windsor, in 1880 (designed by James

F. E. EDBROOKE

Frank Edbrooke in the early 1890s, when the
"palace" hotel he designed for Henry C. Brown
opened in downtown Denver.

COURTESY OF THE COLORADO HISTORICAL SOCIETY, F15322.

Duff), and the Markham Hotel in 1882, which was possibly designed or built by Edbrooke. Both buildings bore unmistakable resemblances to the distinctive Opera House.

Although the other members of the Edbrooke family returned to the East after the Tabor projects, Frank chose to stay and start his own architectural firm. Over the next four decades, Edbrooke's buildings played a significant role in transforming Denver into a real city.

The first buildings known to have been designed by Edbrooke alone were the Navarre building at Broadway and Tremont Place in 1880 and the First Baptist Church at 1747 Stout Street. The Navarre still stands and is on the National Register of Historic Places, but the church was demolished. However, surviving photographs show it to have been a remarkable building, essentially borrowing successful concepts from the Opera House and including a façade of red brick and sharply contrasting limestone over the less-distinguished back of the building and interior.

In 1884 Edbrooke, showing both his growth and his versatility, built a very different type of structure: the Chamber of Commerce building at Fourteenth and Lawrence Streets. Unlike the more flamboyant Opera House and First Baptist Church, the stone-faced Chamber of Commerce building was restrained and orderly—indeed many thought its classic simplicity was its most attractive feature.

Thereafter he created a seemingly unending succession of significant and attractive designs, including these National Register buildings: Joslins Dry Goods at 934 Sixteenth Street, Denver Dry Goods at Sixteenth and California Streets, the Ouray County Courthouse in the town of Ouray, the Masonic Temple at 1614 Welton Street, the Oxford Hotel at 1612 Seventeenth Street, the Central Presbyterian Church at 1660 Sherman Street, the Burlington Hotel at 2205 Larimer Street, Loretto Heights Academy at 3001 South Federal Boulevard, the Hendrie and Bolthoff Warehouse at 1743 Wazee

Street, the Gas and Electric Building at 910 Fifteenth Street, and the early Temple Emanuel building at 2400 Curtis Street.

Yet, impressive as this list is, Edbrooke's reputation as an architect would probably be secure on the basis of a single design he began in 1889. At the request of Henry C. Brown, Edbrooke accepted the commission for the design of a hotel on a difficult triangle of land between Seventeenth Street, Tremont Place, and Broadway. Until that time, few if any notable buildings had been built on such lots. New York City's famous Flatiron Building, for example, was not built until 1902.

Edbrooke was equal to the task. His design for the Brown Palace Hotel remains as popular and memorable today as it was over 100 years ago and is generally considered to be among the finest examples of American commercial architecture. Occupying the entire block, the gently rounded points of the triangle on the granite and sandstone building create a dramatic yet smooth flowing effect. Interestingly, each of the building's three sides incorporated attractive entrances to the building—a decision that gave equal importance, functionally and architecturally, to each facade. Unfortunately, the Broadway entrance was later closed as part of a remodeling effort, which has markedly detracted from the appeal and attractiveness of that side of the building.

Among the other attributes of the building is its large, glass-roofed atrium—believed to be the first use of such a design feature in a hotel. This allowed all guest rooms to be placed facing out, with no airshafts or blocked views.

Edbrooke also designed private houses, including his own at 931 East Seventeenth Street and several others in the Swallow Hill Historic District as well as other sites in the city.

Frank Edbrooke's last building was the Colorado State Museum at Fourteenth Avenue and Sherman Street in the Civic Center Historic District. Oddly, it more closely resembles his Chamber of Commerce Building of thirty-one years earlier than most of his later work, although in white marble and with a more classical design. He retired in 1915 and moved to California for the last six years of his life.

He died in California on May 21, 1921, and his wife, Camilla lived until 1929. However, after his death he was returned to Denver to be buried at Fairmount Cemetery in a private mausoleum. The mausoleum was his own design and, strictly speaking, perhaps it, rather than the Colorado State Museum, was Frank Edbrooke's last building.

One of architect Frank Edbrooke's last designs: his mausoleum at Fairmount Cemetery.

An early studio photograph of **William Henry Jackson** as a young man.

COURTESY OF THE COLORADO HISTORICAL SOCIETY, F43326.

William Henry Jackson's grave
at Arlington National Cemetery.

PHOTO BY JONATHON HALPERIN.

$\mathcal{W}$ILLIAM HENRY JACKSON
1843–1942

William Henry Jackson was one of America's foremost photographers and certainly the best known of those who photographed the West in the nineteenth century. Jackson's meticulously created images, often captured on cumbersome twenty-by-twenty-four-inch negative plates, were among the first glimpses most people had of the West and of Colorado as a territory and a state. The images were both impressive and memorable, and they remain popular today, appearing in John Fielder's "re-photography" classic *Colorado, 1870–2000*.

Jackson was born on April 4, 1843, in Keeseville, New York, on the banks of the Ausable River near Lake Champlain. Photography itself had been invented just four years earlier, and it was to this new craft that Jackson's interest turned as a teenager. He began working as an artist for photography studios in the area, primarily doing hand-retouching and coloring of photographs, but also learning the mechanics, chemistry, and theory of photography. It was a complicated process, involving bulky cameras and wet glass plates of very slow film.

He served with the Union in the Civil War, in a Vermont regiment, then resumed working in photography studios near his home. At the age of twenty-three—perhaps partly as a result of an unhappy romance—Jackson left the Lake Champlain area and eventually made his way to Nebraska. He worked for a while driving oxen for wagon trains before settling in Omaha, where he opened his own photography studio in 1867 and was married in 1869. One of his clients was the Union Pacific Railroad, which wanted a photographic record of its expansion through Nebraska. This provided Jackson with an opportunity to begin perfecting the kind of landscape photography with which he is identified today.

Three years later, in 1870, he came to the attention of Ferdinand Vandiveer Hayden, who was organizing a massive expedition to conduct a geologic survey of the territories west of Nebraska, and it was during the next eight years that Jackson began turning out the series of memorable photographs that would become his best-known artistic legacy.

Jackson's photographs of the Yellowstone area were the first of that region to be published and gave him a national reputation. They also helped attract attention to the area and build support for the movement that culminated in 1872 when Yellowstone became the first national park in the world. Jackson was also part of an expedition to southwestern Colorado, and in 1874 he became the first to photograph the ruins of Mesa Verde. In 1873, Jackson, whose first wife had died in childbirth two years earlier, married Emilie Painter, from Omaha.

As the work of the geological surveys was ending, Jackson opened a photography studio in 1879: the W. H. Jackson Photo Company on Larimer Street in Denver. Jackson never enjoyed the side of the business that involved studio portraits, but he managed to attract many clients who wanted him for his landscape work. Perhaps because of his earlier work for the Union Pacific, Jackson was hired by the Denver and Rio Grande Railroad, for which he took hundreds of photographs for use in advertising and publicity. His work was so successful that he was soon in demand by most other railroads—which were among the largest and most prestigious companies of the day—including the New York Central and Baltimore and Ohio lines. He also began publishing and selling postcards and prints of his extensive collection of Western photos, including perhaps his most famous photograph: Colorado's Mount of the Holy Cross.

By 1894, however, Colorado was in a deep economic depression, and Jackson's clients were cutting back on non-essentials such as expensive photography. Jackson decided to accept a commission to photograph the world's railways, and embarked on a two-year world tour. When he returned to Denver, the depression had ended, but his business was still suffering—in part because of his long absence. In 1897 he decided to move to Detroit, where he joined the Detroit Photographic Company, a leader in a new technology of transforming black-and-white negatives into color prints, and particularly color postcards. Collecting colorized postcards became something of a craze in the early twentieth century. He stayed with the company until its demise in 1924. Although Jackson was by then eighty-one, he continued working—painting, lecturing, and writing—until his death in New York City in 1942 at the age of ninety-nine.

Although he is best-known for photography, Jackson also painted, and he wrote two well-regarded autobiographies: *The Pioneer Photographer: Rocky Mountain Adventures with a Camera,* in 1929, and *Time Exposure: The Autobiography of William Henry Jackson,* in 1940. Both are still in print, and books of his photographs, such as *Gateway Garden of the Gods* and *Pikes Peak, Colorado* and *William Henry Jackson's Rocky Mountain Railroad Album: Steam and Steel across the Great Divide,* are much sought-after by collectors. Many of Jackson's original photographs are in the Western History Collection of the Denver Public Library. His oil paintings and watercolors—going all the way back to sketches he did on the Oregon Trail in the 1860s—are in many museum collections, including the Denver Art Museum, the Smithsonian American Art Museum, and the Scotts Bluff National Monument in Nebraska, which has sixty-three works by Jackson.

He is buried at Arlington National Cemetery in Washington, D.C.

Jennie Rogers.
COURTESY OF THE COLORADO
HISTORICAL SOCIETY, F37953.

$\mathcal{J}$ENNIE ROGERS
1843–1909

Today the 1900 block of Market Street is home to sports bars in Denver's lively "LoDo" neighborhood just around the corner from Coors Field. In the late 1800s Market Street was also a lively place, but it was then called Holladay Street and it was the center of Denver's red light district. The building at what is today 1942 Market Street was home to Jennie Rogers's fabled House of Mirrors, one of the most lavish and expensive houses of prostitution in the West.

Rogers, the future "Queen" of Denver's brothels, was born Leah J. Tehme on July 4, 1843, near Pittsburgh, Pennsylvania. Her early history is largely unknown, but by all accounts she was strikingly attractive. While in her twenties she briefly was married to a Pittsburgh doctor and then had a scandalous affair with the Pittsburgh mayor. After leaving the city she moved in with a riverboat captain named Rogers and, although there is no evidence of a marriage, she adopted his name, which also was the name of his boat—*Jennie Rogers.*

By 1873 the tall, thirty-year-old brunette had moved to St. Louis, Missouri, where she ran what she called "a resort," but which was actually a house of prostitution. In 1879 she left St. Louis, when she apparently encountered some opposition from reform groups, and settled in Denver, which was a comparatively wide-open town.

Her first business was in a small brick building at 527 Holladay Street, today 2009 Market Street, which she bought from another well-known madam, Mattie Silks. Rogers expanded her enterprise to a larger building nearby before finally opening the House of Mirrors, which featured elegant furnishings, mirrored walls and ceilings in the parlor, and perhaps other mirrors strategically placed elsewhere in the building.

Rogers was a good businesswoman and ran a good whorehouse. Always an accomplished rider, she frequently drove through town behind four horses and an open coach carrying and displaying some of her employees, who were customarily referred to as "boarders." Many of Denver's leading citizens were among her clientele, including both elected and appointed government officials, which may explain why the city's red light district managed to flourish openly for so many years despite the existence of laws against prostitution. Although Rogers apparently had ongoing relationships with several prominent people who were also customers of her establishments, there is no evidence that she was a prostitute. Indeed, in the better class of brothels it was thought to be bad for morale for a madam to compete with her employees.

One of Rogers's friends and longtime customers in Denver was a St. Louis policeman, perhaps the St. Louis chief of police according to some unverified sources, whom she had first met when she lived in that city. Rumors abounded that Rogers was not above using blackmail to raise money for her ventures, and one of the most frequently mentioned cases involved Rogers and her St. Louis policeman friend. Various sketchy but colorful accounts state that their target was an aspiring Denver politician whose first wife had conveniently disappeared without a trace, allowing the politician to marry a wealthy woman who could advance his career. As the story goes, Rogers and the policeman dug up an Indian burial site and made off with the skull and some bones of a woman, which they buried in the politician's back yard. Rogers's policeman accomplice confronted the man with the discovery and threatened to alert the local authorities. The man, thinking his wife's remains had been discovered, agreed to pay $17,000 in return for their silence. True or not, it makes a good story.

Meanwhile, in 1881 Rogers met the love of her life, twenty-three-year-old Jack Wood. Their relationship was a stormy one at first. According to an account by Clark Secrest in his book *Hell's Belles,* Rogers once caught Wood with another woman and shot him in the arm, later explaining, memorably and dramatically: "I shot him because I love him, damn him."

Love eventually won out and in 1889 they were married. Together they successfully ran the House of Mirrors until Jack's death in 1896. Rogers, who by then was also using her married

Gravesite of Leah Wood (also known as Jennie Rogers) and her husband, Jack, at Fairmount Cemetery.

name, Leah J. Wood, continued to run the business until 1902 when she came down with a serious kidney disease. Now nearing sixty years of age, her health failing and her looks fading, she moved to Chicago, perhaps to seek better medical care. While she was there she married a contractor named Archie Fitzgerald in 1904, and for the next five years she divided her time between Chicago and Denver, where she died on October 17, 1909, when her chronic disease finally claimed her life. Her estate was valued at $82,000, the equivalent of more than $1 million today. After her death her former competitor, Mattie Silks, bought the House of Mirrors for $14,000, but in 1915 the city finally shut down the brothel business along Market Street.

Rogers was buried at the Fairmount Cemetery gravesite she had built for her and her husband and under a tombstone bearing the name Leah J. Wood. Today, Rogers's old House of Mirrors is a restaurant with a bar named Mattie's Red Light Lounge. The building itself has been restored and bears a plaque proclaiming it as a downtown Denver landmark of a bygone era.

William F. Cody
1846–1917

The popular image of "Buffalo Bill," riding a white horse and wearing fancy clothing, performing in theatrical Wild West shows, often obscures the fact that there was a great deal of substance behind the legend.

William F. Cody was born in Iowa in 1846 but soon moved to Kansas. In 1857, at the age of 11, Cody went to work. It was in 1859, while he was working as a miner and a Pony Express rider, that Cody—then known as "Willie" and barely in his teens—first came to Colorado, joining the many who were looking for gold. He returned to Denver ten years later, chasing cattle thieves for the army. During those years Cody's home remained in Kansas, but he was constantly on the move throughout the west—pausing just long enough in 1866 to marry Louisa Frederici of St. Louis and open a small hotel near Leavenworth, Kansas.

In 1872, during the Indian Wars, he was awarded the Congressional Medal of Honor for gallantry in action with the Army on the Platte River in Nebraska. By that time Cody's real-life Western resumé was an impressive one: cowboy, trapper, miner, member of the Nebraska legislature, scout, wagon train driver, Pony Express rider, decorated soldier, innkeeper, and buffalo hunter. All by the age of twenty-six.

By the late 1860s Cody's remarkable career had attracted the attention of Ned Buntline, a prolific writer of "dime novels." Some say it was Buntline who gave Cody his nickname; others believe that

A classic pose of **William F. "Buffalo Bill" Cody** in a studio portrait. Cody and his horse seem equally in command.
NATE SALSBURY COLLECTION, COURTESY OF THE DENVER PUBLIC LIBRARY, WESTERN HISTORY COLLECTION, NS-27.

"Buffalo Bill" Cody's gravesite on Lookout Mountain, just west of Denver.

he acquired it in a contest with another buffalo hunter, during which, legend has it, Cody killed eleven buffalo with twelve bullets. Whatever the truth, Buntline is responsible for introducing Cody to the world with his 1869 publication of *Buffalo Bill, the King of the Border Men.*

The story was an immediate success and was followed by scores of Buffalo Bill tales—some true, some loosely based on truth, and some outright inventions of Buntline or other writers who followed him. In 1872 a play about Cody debuted in New York, and later that year Cody himself starred in the lead role at the Chicago production of another play: *The Scouts of the Prairie!* (subtitled *And Red Deviltry as it is!*).

Cody took to show business with the same relish he had taken to everything else. Over the next ten years he spent much of his time making public appearances, with occasional interludes to rejoin the army for special assignments—generally serving as a scout for army units that were tracking down increasingly outnumbered bands of Indians. One such tour of duty led to Cody's much-publicized 1876 killing and scalping of a Cheyenne chief in hand-to-hand combat in a retaliatory attack shortly after General Custer's defeat at Little Big Horn. In 1877 he moved to Nebraska, and in 1886 he started a ranch near North Platte, which is today Buffalo Bill Ranch State Historical Park.

It was while Cody was in Nebraska planning a Fourth of July celebration that the idea for a Western show was born. Cody's "Old Glory Blowout" in North Platte in 1882 was probably the first organized rodeo in the world. However, the shows would not become commercially successful until Cody teamed up with a talented New York producer and actor named Nate Salsbury. Their collaboration resulted in the 1884 debut of the enormously successful "Buffalo Bill's Wild West," by any measure one of the longest running shows in entertainment history. The show was built around a huge rodeo featuring a cast of hundreds, including cowboys, Indians, soldiers, buffalo, horses, and cattle in a spectacular mixture of music and parades, rodeo events, and battle reenactments that took America and the world by storm. "Buffalo Bill" became a household name—and Cody became perhaps the most famous person of his era, and deserving of the term "a legend in his own time."

A more thoughtful side of Cody's complex personality also became evident at times during these years as he began speaking out on behalf of issues such as Indian rights and conservation, a cause in which he was joined by his friend Teddy Roosevelt.

The Wild West Show, featuring such draws as Annie Oakley and Sitting Bull, toured for the next three decades—and included trips to Europe, where he performed before Queen Victoria. The show, which was seen by millions, brought Cody fame and fortune. But Nate Salsbury's death in 1902, and some unwise investments by Cody in everything from real estate to mining, eventually brought the Wild West show, and Cody himself, to the brink of bankruptcy.

The end of Cody's financial independence came in Denver in 1913. He was unable to repay a $20,000 loan from *Denver Post* publisher Harry Tammen, who he had known since the 1880s when he became a regular guest at Denver's Windsor Hotel, where Tammen was bartender. To meet his financial obligations Cody toured, unhappily, from 1913 to 1915 with Tammen's Sells-Floto Circus. He received second billing, albeit as "Buffalo Bill Himself," in the troupe, which was renamed the Sells Floto-Buffalo Bill Circus. Down, but not out, he turned to a new medium—motion pictures—and planned to make Western movies based on his adventures.

But Cody's health was failing, and he never was able to implement his planned feature film career. He died of kidney failure in 1917 at the age of 70, while at his sister's house in Denver.

Even in death, he remained the center of attention as Denver boosters and residents of Cody, Wyoming, fought over the famous body. Although Buffalo Bill had always been traveling, he had probably spent as much time in Colorado as in any other place since the

1850s. As for Cody—a town he had founded in 1895 as a land development—his home had been there only since 1911, when he sold his Nebraska ranch to raise money.

Although there was evidence that Cody wanted to be buried in Wyoming, it appears that Denver was able to offer his widow a more attractive financial proposal. Whatever the details, Cody's wife and some of his associates indicated his last wish had been to be buried on a mountaintop near Denver.

And so, after lying in state at the Colorado Capitol, Cody was buried atop Lookout Mountain overlooking Denver. In the eloquent words of *Denver Post* reporter Gene Fowler, it was a site built "to receive the honored body of a modern knight errant, his escutcheon unsullied by selfishness, his record the history of the West."

In 1921 Cody's wife, Louisa, died and was buried alongside her husband. Sporadic efforts by the people of Wyoming and Nebraska to move Buffalo Bill's remains continued for many years—even after Denver officials had added tons of concrete to the gravesite—rendering removal virtually impossible.

Buffalo Bill's grave remains one of the top tourist attractions in Colorado to this day.

John Elitch.
COURTESY OF THE COLORADO
HISTORICAL SOCIETY, 86.296.1061.

Mary Elitch.
COURTESY OF THE COLORADO
HISTORICAL SOCIETY, F34103, F38619.

$\mathcal{J}$OHN ELITCH
1852–1891
$\mathcal{M}$ARY ELITCH LONG
1856–1936

For more than 100 years, one of Denver's most popular attractions was Elitch Gardens, an amusement park at West Thirty-Sixth Avenue and Tennyson Street. In reality, the term "amusement park" is at best an inadequate description of Elitch Gardens. To generation after generation of Coloradans and visitors, Elitch's was much more than that.

The Elitch story began in California in 1872 when sixteen-year-old Mary Hauck eloped with John Elitch, who was twenty. They lived in San Francisco for ten years, where John ran a lunch counter and became interested in the theater, an interest which led to some unsuccessful investments in creating vaudeville acts.

In 1882 they moved to Colorado, where John again went into the restaurant business, running a successful establishment at Fifteenth and Arapahoe Streets in downtown Denver. Profits from the restaurant allowed the Elitches to buy a farm in west Denver. The original idea may have been to use the farm primarily as a home and a source of produce for the restaurant, but they soon began to think of another use for property, with its gardens and orchards and proximity to a streetcar line. By 1888 they had sold the restaurant and began developing what had become their dream: Elitch's Zoological Gardens. Although the zoo remained a part of the operation until the 1930s, at the time the gates opened in 1890 Elitch's was already more than just a zoo. John Elitch had built a theater for vaudeville acts, Mary had started flower gardens, and to attract children there were pony rides and other amusements.

Elitch's was a popular and financial success from the start. During that summer of 1890 the people of Denver quickly made Elitch's a part of their lives.

Less than a year later, however, while on a tour of California with his theatrical group, John Elitch died of pneumonia at the age of 39. The dream almost vanished. Without her husband, Mary Elitch didn't know if she should, or could, continue the venture. His touring company had been expensive, and there was barely enough money left to open Elitch's for a second season, let alone continue to build and grow the Gardens. With just a month to go before the scheduled re-opening, Mary made her decision. She raised money from local investors—who were paid back within three years—and the Gardens re-opened on time.

For the next 26 years, the Gardens grew and flourished under Mary's management. She had remarried in 1900, becoming Mary Elitch Long, but continued to live on the property of the Gardens.

Other amusement parks came to Denver, but none ever seriously threatened to dislodge Elitch's from the hearts of the people. It was a safe, well-maintained, and well-run park—with attractive landscaping, theaters, and restaurants. True to its name, it always seemed to be as much a garden as an amusement park.

Over the years Elitch's entertainment attractions changed significantly. Denver's first movie theater was at Elitch's, and vaudeville gave way to first-rate music, theater, and dancing. The country's first summer stock theater debuted at Elitch's, attracting the biggest names in show business in the early twentieth century: Cecil B. DeMille, Duke Ellington, Helen Hayes, and Douglas Fairbanks, to name just a few.

As Mary neared the age of sixty, the strain of running the business side of Elitch's was beginning to show. Her second husband—who had worked at Elitch's—died in 1906, and over the next few years she found it increasingly difficult to manage the finances.

John K. Mullen, who had made a fortune in the milling business selling Hungarian Flour, had been offering Mary advice and assistance for several years. But by 1916 the situation became critical as bills simply weren't being paid and taxes were in arrears. Mullen and some others notables, including Benjamin Stapleton, later to be mayor of Denver, stepped in. They provided Mary with an investment that kept the Gardens afloat, but also managed to transfer control to the Mullens group. They hired accountant John Mulvihill to

The gravesite of John and Mary Elitch at Fairmount Cemetery.

run the business. He soon acquired a controlling interest from Mullen and he and his family ran the business for the next seventy-eight years. He brought tighter fiscal controls, and eventually got rid of the zoo, but retained most of the qualities that made Elitch's unique, and added some new ones. In the 1930s and 1940s Elitch's famous Trocadero Ballroom became a magnet for young people and attracted most of the marquee names in big bands and swing, including Harry James, Tommy Dorsey, and Gene Krupa.

The Mulvihill family also oversaw the transformation of Elitch's to a modern amusement park, with roller coasters and other mechanized rides.

Mary stayed on the property into the 1930s, and continued to play a meaningful role in the park. As she had from the beginning, she remained active and visible, greeting guests, meeting performers, and helping to tend the gardens and the animals. And the park continued a Mary Elitch innovation: free admission for children on Tuesdays.

She died on July 16, 1936, at her sister's house near Elitch's, where she had moved because of her health in 1932. She was buried with John Elitch at Fairmount Cemetery.

Today, Elitch's survives at another location—although just in name—as Six Flags Elitch Gardens in the Platte Valley of Denver. Six Flags operates thirty-nine parks in the United States and Europe and is the largest regional theme park company.

ℛOBERT WALTER SPEER
1855–1918

Denver's transformation from a frontier town to a city owes much to the entrepreneurs who came to Denver in the late 1800s. However, the driving force behind the public works projects that changed the actual appearance of the city was entrepreneur-turned-politician Mayor Robert W. Speer.

Speer was born in Pennsylvania in 1855; the month and day are not known. He worked for the Pennsylvania Railroad until 1878 when he, like many others, moved to Colorado in an effort to recover from tuberculosis.

Speer's health improved in Colorado and he went to work in Denver at the Fisher store, later Daniels & Fisher. Soon he became active in politics and also sold real estate. He and his wife, Kate, lived in large houses at 505 Clarkson Street and later at 300 Humboldt Street in subdivisions Speer helped create.

In 1884 he became Denver city clerk, and in 1885 he was appointed to be Denver postmaster by President Grover Cleveland. Speer proved to be an effective politician and developed powerful relationships with the people running the city's utilities and with city workers. When he was appointed to the Denver Fire and Police Board in 1891—well before there was any kind of civil service—he was able to use his position to provide jobs in the police and fire departments to supporters. The use of patronage to increase his power base was repeated in 1901 when the forty-six-year-old Speer became head of the city's largest agency, the Board of Public Works.

Flashing his best campaign smile, a beaming **Mayor Speer** is pictured in this early 1900s photograph.

THE HARRY M. RHOADS PHOTOGRAPH COLLECTION, COURTESY OF
THE DENVER PUBLIC LIBRARY, WESTERN HISTORY COLLECTION, RH862.

By most accounts, the quality of the city government of Denver in the late 1800s was—at best—uneven. Indeed, the situation had gotten so bad that in the 1890s the state intervened, and took control of much of the city government. Unfortunately, there was little evidence that the state's efforts resulted in any significant improvements and after 1900 efforts intensified to achieve true "home rule" for Denver. An early home rule charter proposal, supported by the "reform" elements in the city, was defeated—opposed by Speer and his associates, including William Gray Evans, head of the Denver Tramway Company and son of Territorial Governor John Evans. It was not until 1902 that a charter acceptable to Speer and the city's business leaders was adopted. Article XX of the Colorado Constitution, consolidated Denver City with several small towns in the area—such as Globeville and Montclair—into a single, unified City and County of Denver, with full home rule.

The first mayor elected under the new charter was Speer himself. He would serve from 1904 to 1912, and from 1916 to 1918: terms of both controversy and achievement. The Speer years were characterized by continual political warfare between the mayor and his supporters, on the one hand, and a group of "good government" advocates on the other. The group of Speer's opponents included fellow Democrats Judge Ben Lindsey, Senator Thomas Patterson, and Ed Costigan, a lawyer and a leader of Denver's liberal community. Denver's two major newspapers, one of which was owned by Patterson, were also hostile to Speer—charging that his administration was characterized by cronyism, corruption, and crime.

In retrospect, and despite his shortcomings, Speer not only had many supporters in the city, but also managed to accomplish a great deal. He was certainly not a political reformer, but he was strongly devoted to a different kind of reform: re-forming Denver from a dusty eyesore to an attractive, livable, and efficient city. Speer was an enthusiastic proponent of city planning and an urban architectural movement called the "City Beautiful," which favored massive public projects such as New York's Central Park, Chicago's Columbian Exposition, and Cleveland's Civic Center.

Under Speer, and his Denver Art Commission, Denver received the "City Beautiful" treatment. Speer's many successful projects included cleaning up Cherry Creek, which was essentially an open sewer at the time; building Cherry Creek Drive—renamed Speer Boulevard in 1910; building the Civic Center and a large auditorium; doubling the city's park acreage; and erecting bridges, paving streets, building playgrounds, installing sidewalks, planting trees, and burying the tangle of overhead wiring that provided phone and electric service. At a time when Denver had no real zoning laws, Speer favored curbs on private development, including limiting building height and restricting billboards. He even began planning for Denver's future, foreseeing the mountain parks program and the City and County Building.

But the drumbeat of opposition to "Boss" Speer's political tactics eventually had their effect. He decided not to seek re-election in 1912. In an effort to prevent what were seen as the excesses of the Speer mayoralty, a city charter amendment was passed in 1913 changing Denver's government from a strong-mayor system to a commission system, with most power residing in the elected commissioners.

The attempt at reform backfired. Not only did Speer supporters win several of the commission seats, but one of the men, who replaced Speer as mayor, Henry J. Arnold, decided—after taking office—that he too preferred a strong-mayor form of government. In 1916 the commission experiment was scrapped in favor of another strong-mayor charter, and the strong mayor who was elected in that year was again . . . Robert W. Speer.

Feeling vindicated by his 1916 re-election, Speer picked up where he had left off in 1912. The Civic Center project, which had languished in his absence, was reinvigorated, and he accelerated the effort to create a system of Denver mountain parks. However, Speer never got to see the completion of many of his visions for Denver as a "City Beautiful." Just two years into his new term as mayor he contracted pneumonia and died on May 14, 1918. He is buried at Fairmount Cemetery.

Many of Speer's unfinished plans were realized under his successors, notably long-time mayor Ben Stapleton who made good use of federal "New Deal" funding in the 1930s to complete projects Speer had begun. Denver's Mountain Parks now cover more than twenty-two square miles, including thirty-one parks and sixteen wilderness areas in Jefferson, Douglas, Clear Creek, and Grand counties. And, it would be fourteen years after Speer's death, and more than twenty years after the idea had first been proposed, that Denver's City and County Building was opened on August 1, 1932. Speer's widow, Kate, donated the money for the clock and bell in the tower of the building that anchored the Civic Center, which became an unofficial memorial to her husband's vision for a livable and attractive city.

The grave of Denver's twenty-fifth and twenty-ninth mayor, Robert W. Speer, in Fairmount Cemetery.

Enos Mills in 1915 at Estes Park.
COURTESY OF THE DENVER PUBLIC LIBRARY,
WESTERN HISTORY COLLECTION, Z106.

The back of Enos Mills's original cabin, near Estes
Park. In all probability, Mills initially was interred
behind the cabin; later he was cremated and his ashes
were scattered nearby.

$\mathcal{E}$NOS ABIJAH MILLS
1870–1922

Today there are almost 400 areas administered by the National Park Service, and it is easy for attractions such as the Rocky Mountain National Park (RMNP) to be taken for granted. Yet at one time the future of such unique areas was very much in doubt, and there was considerable pressure to allow unregulated development by commercial interests. The existence of these parks is due in great measure to the efforts of a handful of naturalists who were born in the nineteenth century. One of these individuals was Enos Mills of Estes Park, Colorado.

Mills was born in 1870 in southeastern Kansas. As a child his health was poor, including digestive ailments that probably included an allergy to wheat. In 1884, at the age of fourteen, Mills left home and traveled to Colorado, which was widely believed to have a healthy climate. Mills had several relatives living in Colorado at the time, including an uncle who was a preacher in Estes Park.

Mills took to the mountains with a passion. He made the first of hundreds of ascents of Long's Peak in 1885, and thereafter worked as a guide for the mountain for the next two decades, primarily during the summer tourist season. His first few winters in Colorado were spent working on ranches at lower elevations; by summertime he was always back in the mountains, working on a small homestead cabin ten miles south of Estes Park, and employed at tourist lodges such as the Elkhorn or Long's Peak House, which was owned by his uncle.

Today, Mills's mountain climbing technique would be called

"extreme light backpacking." He eschewed most equipment, including tents and heavy blankets or specialized clothing, and generally headed into the mountains for days at a time and in all kinds of weather with little more than a felt hat, a pair of hobnail boots, a light jacket, and work clothes. Mills's food supply often consisted of a pocketful of raisins, which could last for several days.

Mills required little in the way of creature comforts; he preferred traveling as lightly as possible and with little to separate him from his environment, including animals such as beavers and grizzly bears, which he loved.

Beginning in 1887, and for most of the next fifteen years, Mills's primary source of income was his seasonal work in mines, particularly the large Anaconda Mine in Butte, Montana. Mills became a skilled mineworker, and his salary was substantially greater than his income at the lodges. Mills's earnings went into his purchase of Long's Peak House, which he bought from his uncle and which opened as Long's Peak Inn under his ownership in 1902. He continued to operate it until his death twenty years later.

Mills's interest in the environment was accelerated by a chance meeting with John Muir in 1889, when Muir was in the midst of the battle to acquire national park status for the Yosemite area. Both men shared a natural affinity for the outdoors and a desire to spend as much time as possible enjoying it. However, their environmental perspectives differed significantly; Muir was more of a purist than Mills and would have preferred virtually no human incursion into the wilderness. Mills, on the other hand, accepted tourism and believed it could provide great economic benefits for Colorado. His overriding priority was to make sure that areas of great natural beauty were saved *for* tourists to enjoy, not sealed off *from* them. The difference between Mills and Muir was underscored by Mills's careers as a miner, as an innkeeper, and as an employee for the Forest Service and other federal agencies. Muir regarded these agencies as the enemy, an opinion that would eventually be adopted by Mills as well. Mills was also an ardent supporter of the conservation initiatives of President Theodore Roosevelt. To Muir, Roosevelt's forest reserve plans were little more than giveaways to the private interests of loggers and others. Mills himself worked for Roosevelt as a forest policy spokesman from 1907 to 1909.

By 1905 Mills's life was centered almost exclusively in Estes Park, and he began lecturing and writing books and articles extolling the area. He soon achieved a national reputation as a promoter of Estes Park and as a spokesman for the growing conservation movement.

His Long's Peak Inn became a popular resort, and Mills himself often led climbing and hiking expeditions. The lodge reflected Mills's ascetic personality. Although the food was quite good, the atmosphere was reserved. Such resort activities as music and dancing were not allowed; quiet and tranquility prevailed. The lodge prospered and attracted scores of celebrities and famous people.

Mills's rise to national prominence coincided with conflicts over the issues of development and conservation with members of his family and with friends and associates. To them Mills seemed to have become overly ambitious and opinionated, and for the remainder of his life he increasingly would be viewed by some as a controversial and contentious individual.

By 1910, when the Stanley Hotel opened, Estes Park was one of the nation's most popular destination resorts. At that time there was no national park and there were few obstacles to commercial development. Tourist facilities and attractions were everywhere, including in areas that are today within RMNP.

It was at this time that some in Estes Park began exploring ways to preserve the beauty of the area while continuing to attract tourists. Some advocated creating a game preserve, while others, including Mills, favored a national park. However, the term "national park" was still vague and not clearly defined. There was as yet no uniform park system; indeed there was not even a National Park Service. All of the parks that had been created up to that time—Yosemite, Yellowstone, Mesa Verde, and the others—were informally managed by the Department of the Interior.

It was within this context that the discussion of the creation of the RMNP took place. There were many supporters, including the railroads and most of the tourism community in the area including industrialist F. O. Stanley, owner of the town's biggest hotel. However, Mills soon became the most active and visible champion of the RMNP, writing books, lecturing, and lobbying throughout the country at his own expense. Opponents included the Forest Service, which wanted the area to be run as a game preserve under Forest Service control, and loggers, miners, ranchers, and settlers, who wanted private development and homesteading in the area.

In 1912 the Interior Department sent a representative to evaluate the proposed park site, and his report was strongly supportive. Also joining the pro-park forces was James Grafton Rogers, an influential Denver lawyer and a member of the Colorado Mountain Club, who began writing the legislation that would create the park.

Rogers's first proposal included an attempt to attract broader support by appearing to allow mining, grazing, and logging to take place. While seemingly at odds with what most people felt a park should be, Rogers had concluded that in fact the proposed park had few if any such resources in commercially usable quantities. What seemed like a concession to commercial interests in fact offered them few real benefits.

Unfortunately, it was difficult to discuss openly this kind of Machiavellian reasoning and clever planning. Mills and others opposed such language on principle, and the bill failed in large part because it was taken at face value as being insufficiently protective of the area. In the course of this debate, the argument between Mills and Grafton became heated and personal, particularly on the part of Mills.

By 1914 the bill had been revised, reducing the size of the park and compromising on the portions of the park that had already been settled. Most homesteads were allowed to remain but not expand. Commercial establishments were allowed to remain until a policy shift in the 1930s led to their buy-out and elimination.

In late 1914 Mills testified before Congress, which finally passed the bill early in 1915. RMNP officially began its existence on January 26, 1915, and from that time forward Mills was often referred to as "the father of Rocky Mountain National Park," much as John Muir, who died in 1914, had been called "the father of National Parks."

In 1916 Congress passed legislation setting up a National Park Service. Mills, who by this time was the nation's best-known national parks advocate, soon became a leading spokesmen for the new agency. Yet by 1919 Mills and the park service had parted company as a result of Mills's public attacks against policies he disliked, including a failure by the Park Service to expand the park boundaries and the granting of monopoly concessions to businesses to operate within the park, an issue which continues to be controversial to this day.

Mills and his allies went to court unsuccessfully to challenge the park's monopoly concession practices, particularly in the area of providing transportation. Political tactics were also tried, but also met with failure—and frequently with heavy-handed threats by the federal government to simply close down the parks.

Mills's first—and only—known serious romantic interest came into his life in 1916 when Esther Burnell, a twenty-seven-year-old interior decorator from Ohio, came to Estes Park as a tourist with her sister. She had apparently heard Mills speak on one of his lecture tours and wanted to see the new park for herself. Burnell fell in love with the region, got a job as a typist for Mills, and staked a homestead claim, where she built a home on 160 acres. She had also taken Mills's teachings to heart and spent most of her free time exploring the mountains. It soon became evident that Mills's interest in Burnell went beyond her skills as a typist and had become a romantic one. After a year's courtship, the two were married in August 1918 at Mill's original cabin, although they lived at a newer house nearby. They were soon joined by Mills's only child, a daughter named Enda, who was born in April 1919.

Other than Mills's continuing feud with the federal government over park management policies, the years following his marriage were apparently happy and productive. The Long's Peak Inn continued to expand and to thrive. Mills authored several more well-received books about nature and animals, and he delighted in having a daughter to take for walks in the woods and to teach all the things that were important to him.

After years of risk-taking in the mountains—including sliding down avalanches, playing with bears, and survival camping in sub-freezing conditions—the beginning of Mills's untimely decline appears to have occurred on a New York subway. He was in New York in 1922 for a lecture when the subway on which he was riding had a small collision, throwing him to the floor and breaking a rib. The injury weakened him but initially did not appear to be serious. However it often is blamed—somewhat mysteriously—as the beginning of a downward spiral that led to his death eight months later.

Shortly after his return from New York to Colorado he became very ill with influenza and then underwent oral surgery for a badly infected abscess. Although he was up and around on September 20, 1922, that evening he went into a coma and died in the early morning hours the following day. He was fifty-two.

The cause of death has never been conclusively determined. The coroner apparently believed he had suffered a heart attack; his dentist feared that the cause might have been infection from the abscess.

Fittingly, Mills's well-attended funeral was held at his old cabin. The headlines in the *Denver Post* read:

Buried in Mountain Crypt in Light of Setting Sun.

Casket Lies Before Flickering Log Fire While Nature Poems Are Read as Only Sermon, and his Body Lowered Into Ground to Sound of Moaning Wind.

A columnist, summing up Mills's life, referred to him as one of the trinity of "America's great naturalists," along with John Muir and John Burroughs. Based on Mills's often-expressed admiration for both men, he would have appreciated the association, and he had certainly come to agree with Muir about the evils of the federal land management agencies.

Neither the story of Mills nor the story of his burial ends in 1922. His descendants continue to advance the ideas Mills advocated, and their Enos Mills Cabin Museum and Gallery remains a popular tourist attraction in the Estes Park area to this day. More than twenty books written by Mills are still available at the museum, and many are also available at other bookstores.

Curiously, on the Enos Mills Cabin website there is a different story about Mills's burial from that in either the contemporary newspapers or Alexander Drummond's thorough biography of Mills, *Enos Mills: Citizen of Nature.* The website mentions nothing about burial at the cabin and states that Mills was cremated. His family indicates that his ashes "were spread far and wide."

The truth probably is that he first was buried at the cabin, then exhumed and cremated by the family, maybe fearing vandals—or perhaps they were belatedly honoring Mills's own wishes. In any event, families are entitled to privacy in such matters.

The photograph is of Mills's original cabin and probable initial burial site, which in all likelihood is also the area in which Mills's ashes were scattered by his family.

Adolph Coors.

COURTESY OF THE COLORADO
HISTORICAL SOCIETY, F36127.

The Coors family gravesite at
Crown Hill Cemetery.

*A*DOLPH HERMAN JOSEPH COORS
1847–1929

In 1873, a twenty-six-year-old German immigrant, who had been orphaned at the age of fifteen and only managed to get to the United States as a stowaway on a ship, began brewing beer on the banks of Clear Creek in Golden, Colorado.

Adolph Kohrs, as his name was then, was born in Wuppertal, Prussia, in 1847 and went to work at the age of thirteen, first as a printer's assistant then, fortuitously, as an apprentice in a brewery. His parents died in 1862, but he continued at the brewery, where he learned both the financial and the brewing aspects of the business and became a salaried employee in 1865.

In 1868 Coors, then twenty-one, joined a wave of Germans immigrating to the United States as a result of war and political unrest. In Coors's case, immigrating meant stowing away on a transatlantic ship because he lacked the money for the fare. When he arrived in Baltimore he was broke, spoke almost no English, and had to work to pay back the money he owed for his passage to the United States.

In 1869 he moved west and worked at a management level at the Joseph Stenger Brewery near Chicago. In 1872 he moved on to Colorado, where he worked at several jobs and owned a small bottling company while looking for an opportunity to start a brewery. With the help of local investor Jacob Schueler, who was impressed by Coors, he got the chance two years later and started the small "Golden Brewery." He was attracted to the site, which was originally a tannery, because of the abundance of good water available in Clear

Creek. In later years this water was featured in advertising and marketing as the "pure, Rocky Mountain spring water" that was supposed to give Coors its taste. From the beginning, Adolph Coors and his successors would stress the importance of the quality of the water in the brewing process. Even after they had expanded beyond the original source of Rocky Mountain spring water, and the claim of the water's Colorado origin had disappeared from the label, they continued to seek out what they believed to be high-quality water sources.

Coors was a good businessman, and the company was successful virtually from the start. By 1880 he felt settled enough to get married, and affluent enough to buy out his partner, Schueler. He now owned the company outright and renamed it Coors Golden Brewery.

Coors and his wife, Louise, had six children. Many of them worked in the family business. Coors beer grew rapidly into a strong regional brand until 1916—when prohibition came to Colorado and 1920—when the ban on alcoholic beverages became nationwide. More than half of the breweries in the United States went out of business before prohibition was repealed fourteen years later.

But Coors proved that he was not only a good brewer, but also a shrewd businessman. He had successfully expanded the company into other businesses: cement, malted milk, an alcohol-free product known as Mannah "near-beer," and, in 1910, a stake in Herold China and Pottery Company, which made oven-safe porcelain.

Adolph Coors never lived to see the company emerge from the days of prohibition, although his diversification of the product line provided it with the means for survival. On June 5, 1929, while in Virginia Beach, Virginia, Coors died in a fall from a sixth floor hotel window. There was no inquest, and the incident was reported as an "accidental drop" at the time. According to Dan Baum, in his book *Citizen Coors*, it was suicide—a family tragedy that would be recalled thirty-one years later when his grandson, Adolph "Ad" Coors III, was the victim of a notorious kidnapping and murder.

In later years the Coors name would again be in the news regarding subjects unrelated to brewing. The Coors family, and particularly Bill and Joe Coors, became embroiled in political controversies for their support of conservative causes—including their role in the career and presidency of Ronald Reagan. Subsequent Coors management, representing both family members and outsiders, would successfully soften the political agenda in deference to the necessities of being a publicly held corporation.

Due to the enterprise and astuteness of Adolph Coors and his heirs, Coors's "Golden Brewery" survived and prospered–growing from approximately 100 barrels in 1873 to 100,000 barrels annually at the time of prohibition to more than 20 million barrels per year today. Coors, which merged with Canada's Molson Brewing in 2005, is the third largest brewer in the United States, with a market capitalization of more than $2 billion, and more than 10,000 employees producing what is certainly Colorado's most famous product. And the little porcelain business that Adolph Coors bought back in 1910 eventually became Coors Porcelain, then Coors Ceramics, and finally CoorsTek, a successful high-technology company selling products for the semiconductor market and for industrial, telecommunication, electronic, automotive, and other applications. CoorsTek itself employs almost 2,500 people and has offices throughout the world. Although it was briefly a public company, CoorsTek was re-acquired by the Coors family in 2002 and is now privately held.

Adolph Coors and his wife, who died in 1941, are buried in a family area at Crown Hill Cemetery in Lakewood.

Charles Boettcher in 1902, at the age of fifty.

Boettcher family vault at
Fairmount Mausoleum.

CHARLES BOETTCHER
1852–1948

By the time Charles Boettcher died in 1948, he had traveled far and accomplished much since his birth in Kolleda, Germany, ninety-six years earlier. His life coincided with—and indeed helped bring about—the transformation of Denver from a small mining camp on the banks of Cherry Creek to a major city. Boettcher had an uncanny knack for identifying opportunities and capitalizing on them quickly and decisively.

Boettcher first came to the area to visit a brother in Cheyenne in 1869 at the age of seventeen. He decided to stay, and he operated a series of businesses in Cheyenne, Greeley, Ft. Collins, Leadville, Boulder, and finally, Denver. Although mining was a dominant industry in Colorado at the time, and Boettcher acquired some mining properties in Leadville, his core businesses thrived by selling hardware and other merchandise to the miners and others. While the miners were chasing their dreams, his motto was "Hard Goods. Hardware. Hard Cash."

In 1874 he married Fannie Augusta Cowen. He was twenty-two, she was twenty. At the time his home was at 925 Pearl Street in Boulder, and it was there that a son, Claude, was born in 1875. Claude would carry on and expand the Boettcher businesses.

By 1890 the Boettchers had moved to Denver, building a mansion at 1201 Grant Street in what was called "Millionaire's Row" in the Capitol Hill neighborhood. It was there that a daughter, Ruth, was born.

Boettcher's varied business interests continued to multiply, and included meatpacking, banking, ranching, and real estate. In 1900, having made what would be the first of several fortunes, he decided to retire—a decision that would last all of six months and was, in fact, forty-eight years premature. During his brief retirement he took his family on a "Grand Tour" of Europe. It was while Boettcher was visiting his native Germany that he became interested in the German sugar beet and cement industries. He returned to Denver with some sugar beet seeds, machinery, and ideas about bringing those businesses to Colorado. Retirement was over.

Soon sugar beet crops were thriving in the state, and the Great Western Sugar Company was organized with Boettcher as president. Simultaneously, he launched the Portland (Ideal) Cement Company, near Canon City. He was a backer of David Moffat's ill-fated Denver and Northwestern Railway, and Boettcher and Lawrence C. Phipps guided the company through receivership after Moffat's death. In 1915 Boettcher became president of the successor Denver and Salt Lake Railroad, which eventually merged with the Denver and Rio Grande Western.

In 1912 he sold his meatpacking business to Swift and Company. He owned, or was a principal investor, in a long list of other Colorado businesses, including Capitol Life Insurance Company, Public Service Company, the Denver National Bank, and the invest-ment banking firm of Boettcher, Porter & Co.

By 1919, when Boettcher's daughter Ruth married Albert E. Humphreys, Jr., in the social event of the year, the Boettcher mar-riage had failed. Some say the last straw in the relationship was Fannie's decision to build an expensive sunporch as a backdrop for her daughter's wedding, a decision the thrifty Charles resisted. Charles reportedly said he would leave if the addition took place. Unmoved, Fannie ordered construction to begin. Whatever the cause, Charles moved out—first to The Denver Club, then to the

Brown Palace Hotel, never to return to 1201 Grant. He became a joint owner of the Brown Palace in 1922, where he lived for much of the remainder of his life. He also built a large summer home on a sixty-two-acre site near Lookout Mountain, now part of the Jefferson County parks system.

On the morning of February 13, 1933, Boettcher's grandson, thirty-two-year-old Charles Boettcher II, was kidnapped from his home at 777 Washington Street and held for ransom. According to news reports, the crime was committed by Verne Sankey, of South Dakota, who held his victim at a ranch near Gann Valley, South Dakota, for seventeen days until a $60,000 ransom was paid by the elder Boettcher. Sankey, variously described as a "1930s gangster" and "Public Enemy Number One" and rumored to have been involved in several other notorious high-profile kidnappings, hanged himself in a South Dakota jail about a year after the crime. Tragedy struck the Boettcher family again when, in 1941, Charles Boettcher II's wife, Anna Lou, thirty-seven, killed herself at the Boettcher home.

Charles Boettcher stayed active in business and, increasingly, in philanthropy. He died in 1948 at the age of ninety-six. Fannie lived quietly, managed her own investments and charities, and died in 1952 at the age of ninety-eight. They are buried in a family vault in the mausoleum at Fairmount Cemetery.

Boettcher, his son Claude—who died in 1957 and is buried along with his parents—and their families left an enduring and substantial legacy, including the Boettcher Foundation, which was created in 1937 and is the fifth largest foundation in Colorado.

Dora Moore.
COURTESY OF DORA MOORE K-8 SCHOOL
AND T. JASON MARTINEZ, PRINCIPAL.

$\mathcal{D}$ORA M. MOORE
1855–1938

A woman who spent virtually her entire quiet, unassuming life as a teacher and principal at an elementary school may seem an unusual subject for this book. However, such people represent many others in Colorado and elsewhere—teachers, nurses, police, and firefighters, for example, whose jobs are critical to our society. And many of these people manage to bring something special to their jobs and make enormous, if unsung, contributions to their corners of the world.

In fairness, this teacher is not really unknown. There is an unusually attractive school building on the north side of Eighth Avenue between Corona and Downing Streets in Denver—the Dora Moore School for kindergarten through eighth grade. The building, which was renovated in 2003, is listed on the National Register of Historic Places. It was named after a remarkable woman who taught in Denver for almost half a century and who, in a quiet and effective way, made significant contributions to the lives of thousands of Denver children and families.

Dora M. Moore was born in Ohio in 1855, the daughter of Avery Moore, who worked for a railroad. She decided at an early age that she wanted to be a teacher and never had any second thoughts. Her family moved to Chicago and she graduated with honors from Chicago Normal School, a teaching institution, in 1877. She taught in Chicago public schools for the next two years, before moving to Denver with her father and sister in 1881.

Her first teaching job in Denver was at Ebert School near downtown Denver. In 1890 she moved from her house at 1927 Logan Street to a new house at what was then 1027 Venice Street, later renamed Emerson Street. It was close to the place where she would spend the greater part of her professional career. She left Ebert in 1891 and transferred to the new Corona School, just a few blocks from her new home. In 1893 she was named principal.

For the next thirty-eight years, Moore headed the Corona School, through whose doors passed many of the children from Capitol Hill and east-central Denver neighborhoods, including people such as former First Lady Mamie Eisenhower, former Denver mayors Bill McNichols and Quigg Newton, and former Colorado governor Steve McNichols, who recalled Moore as being "the classic cameo of the pioneer woman—rather severe." She also headed the Colorado Education Association for a term and was active in a variety of charitable and church activities. Although it is difficult to recapture from a century ago what distinguished Moore's career, perhaps some understanding can be gained by a story from the May 7, 1903, issue of the *Denver Republican* newspaper. The remarkable article relates how a group of mothers of children who had attended Corona School since Moore's arrival in 1891 had gotten together to raise money to send her on an all-expense-paid trip to Europe "in appreciation for her services as a teacher." The article noted Moore's astonishment at the gift and pointed out that under normal circumstances, such a trip was well beyond the financial resources of most public school teachers. The article added "as principal, Miss Moore has had the love of the children and the confidence of their parents and the women who have made it possible for her to have such a splendid rest after so many years of work say the gift does not half express their appreciation of her."

In 1929, at the age of seventy-four, Moore retired as principal. So considerable had been her impact on education in Denver that to mark her retirement the school where she had worked for almost four decades was renamed the Dora M. Moore School. At her retirement, Moore had an opportunity to explain her devotion to a life of teaching for fifty consecutive years: "From these children I gain vitality and enthusiasm and hope for each day's work. What I have gained from my long service as teacher is an ever-deepening love of, and faith in, humanity. Especially that portion of humanity we call Youth. They know the way and will not be deceived."

In failing health in the 1930s, after suffering a broken hip, Moore died in her sleep at her home on March 25, 1938. She had never married, and her only survivors were three cousins. She was buried at Fairmount Cemetery, although her memorial, the school, remains on Eighth Avenue in Denver.

Dora Moore School has continued to prosper under more than a dozen principals who followed Moore, and has a large and loyal group of parents, alumni, and friends. In 1990 these friends, along with the school's Parent Teacher Student Association, commissioned a history of the school, *100 Moore Years,* written by veteran Denver journalist Clé Cervi.

Gravesite of Dora Moore at the Fairmount Cemetery.

Fred Bonfils.
COURTESY OF THE DENVER CENTER
FOR THE PERFORMING ARTS.

Helen Bonfils.
COURTESY OF THE DENVER CENTER
FOR THE PERFORMING ARTS.

Mary "May" Bonfils Stanton.
COURTESY OF THE DENVER PUBLIC LIBRARY,
WESTERN HISTORY COLLECTION, F25957.

FREDERICK GILMER BONFILS
1860–1933
HELEN GILMER BONFILS
1889–1972
MARY MADELINE "MAY" BONFILS STANTON
1883–1962

Frederick Gilmer Bonfils was born on December 21, 1860, in Troy, Missouri. As a young man he entered the U.S. Military Academy, but dropped out before graduating. He moved to Kansas City, Missouri, where he was living in 1895 when he joined with Harry Heye Tammen to buy the struggling *Denver Post* newspaper. Details about Bonfils's early background are few. According to Denver newsman Gene Cervi, no admirer of Bonfils, he "amassed his millions through a Kansas lottery, selling nonexistent Oklahoma land, selling coal to reluctant merchants and running a Denver burlesque house."

Whatever the truth about Bonfils's background, the *Post* prospered under the Bonfils–Tammen team. It became the first newspaper successfully to challenge the *Rocky Mountain News*, which had been founded in 1859. The *Post–News* duel was intense and long lasting. By the turn of the nineteenth century, the *Post* was winning the circulation war; however, the battle would go on for all of the next century until a truce of sorts was declared in 2000 with a Joint Operating Agreement between the two dailies.

The *Post's* recipe for competing with the *News* was a steady diet of promotions and sensational journalism augmented, according to some observers, by ruthless business tactics, including threatening to print unfavorable stories about businesses that didn't advertise in the *Post*. Like many other newspapers of the time, the *Post* adopted a muckraking style, going after real or alleged targets involving crime or corruption. The owners adopted the slogan "O Justice, when expelled from other habitations, make this thy dwelling place," which they had inscribed above the door of the *Post* building.

Although Bonfils was known to some among his family and his few friends as having a kind and generous side to his personality, he was also quick to take offense and to anger, and given to printing stories that angered others. As a result, the Bonfils era at the *Post* was not only colorful but violent.

In 1900 Bonfils got into a heated argument with attorney William Anderson. Bonfils felt Anderson had acted in bad faith while on an assignment from the *Post* to try to get convicted cannibal Alfred Packer released from prison—a *Post* publicity stunt. Screaming at Anderson, Bonfils called him a liar, threatened to initiate disbarment proceedings, then physically attacked him and threw him out of the *Post's* office. But Anderson had a gun, and he proceeded to shoot both Bonfils and Tammen at close range. The wounds were serious but not fatal, and both men were soon back at work. Anderson was charged with assault, and many in the community who hated the *Post* rallied to Anderson's side. After three trials—and a guilty plea by Tammen to charges of jury tampering—Anderson was acquitted of the charges on grounds of self-defense.

In 1907, The *Post–News* feud took an even uglier turn. United States Senator Thomas Patterson was editor and publisher of the *News*, and late in December of that year the *News* alleged that the *Post's* business tactics amounted to blackmail and published a cartoon in which Bonfils was depicted as the notorious pirate Captain Kidd.

A few days later, both Patterson and Bonfils were separately walking to work when their paths crossed at Thirteenth Avenue and Logan Street. Bonfils assaulted Patterson, who was struck in the face and fell to the ground. Although Bonfils was convicted of assault and ordered to pay a small fine, Patterson's testimony at the trial was lacking in hard evidence of specific blackmailing acts on the part of Bonfils.

Bonfils also got into a scrape with a local attorney who was working for a water franchise extension. The *Post* opposed the extension and sued. When the lawyer saw Bonfils in the courthouse on the morning of the trial, he tried to pull his gun. Bonfils was too quick and was able to subdue the attorney with his fists.

Despite, or perhaps in part because of, such events, the *Post's* circulation increased, and by the 1920s it was outselling the *News* by more than three to one.

Bonfils and Tammen also owned the *Kansas City Post,* which had been purchased in 1909. As in Denver, business dealings were personal and very intense in Kansas City. Bonfils disliked William Rockhill Nelson, owner of the larger *Kansas City Star,* who he believed was the source of the stories about his illicit lotteries in the days when he lived in Missouri.

Although they followed much the same journalism formula in Kansas City as they had in Denver, the *Kansas City Post* failed to compete successfully against the *Star*. Bonfils and Tammen finally sold the Kansas City paper in 1922, although they ended up having to pay a sizeable judgment as a result of a lawsuit against them for a 1921 story that alleged that two managers at the rival *Star* had engaged in covert pro-German activities during World War I.

In 1922 Bonfils made the first of the family's many major philanthropic gestures, donating seventeen acres at Ninth Avenue and Colorado Boulevard in Denver to the University of Colorado as the site for the medical school campus. Over the years, the family continued to support the medical center.

Fred Bonfils died in 1933. Although his success as a publisher was beyond dispute, one contemporary observer remarked that there were "few to mourn his passing." His wife, Belle, died in 1935, and both are buried in a family vault at the Fairmount Mausoleum. But the Bonfils–*Post* connection endured for thirty-five more years, carried forth by the next generation of Bonfils.

Fred and Belle Bonfils had two daughters, and their younger daughter, Helen, gained control of the paper after her parents' deaths. "Miss Helen," as she was often called, was a stylish and forceful woman, with theatrical interests that would later influence some of her philanthropic gifts to Denver's performing arts community.

During her memorable tenure at the *Post*, she directed that two dozen yellow roses be placed in the *Post's* lobby, to greet her when she

Bonfils family vault at the Fairmount Mausoleum, where Fred Bonfils, his wife, Belle, and his daughter Helen are entombed.

arrived at the paper. In the early years she usually arrived in an elegant Pierce Arrow automobile bearing the Colorado license plate #1.

Under her father, the *Post* was financially successful, but its journalistic reputation was uneven at best. In 1946 Helen Bonfils brought in E. Palmer Hoyt as editor. The paper began to improve, and by the time Hoyt retired in 1970 it was generally regarded as one of the country's better and more influential regional newspapers. Bonfils also took steps to improve wages and benefits at the paper where, under her father, reporters and others had been treated less than generously. Like her father, she became one of Denver's leading philanthropists. She established the Belle Bonfils Blood Bank in memory of her mother and the Bonfils Tumor Clinic in memory of her father. She funded the building of the Holy Ghost Church at 1900 California Street in Denver and was a major supporter of the Denver Zoo, the Denver Dumb Friends League, and many other institutions, including churches and synagogues throughout the area.

But her first passion was the theater, highlighted by her experiences as a Broadway producer and performer. She co-produced *Sleuth*, which won the 1971 Tony Award for best play, and also Noel Coward's 1962 Broadway musical *Sail Away*. In Denver, she built a successful theater on Colfax Avenue, supported many local arts efforts, and ran Elitch's well-regarded theater.

In 1936 Helen, who was then forty-seven, entered into her first marriage. She wed George Somnes, who she met when he was producing plays at the Elitch Theater. The marriage lasted until Somnes's death in 1956.

It was while working on Broadway that Helen met Donald Seawell, a New York theatrical lawyer and producer who represented many of the leading Broadway names of the day, including Noel Coward, Alfred Lunt, Lynn Fontanne, Tallulah Bankhead, Howard Lindsay, and Russel Crouse. As a producer, Seawall's credits included both London and New York productions, including *A Thurber*

Carnival, The Affair, The Beast in Me, Slow Dance on the Killing Ground, several Shakespeare productions, as well as television shows and motion pictures.

Bonfils and Seawell got along well, and in addition to partnering with him to produce several shows and other ventures she began using him as an attorney for herself and for the newspaper. In 1966, facing a potential battle for control of the paper, she persuaded Seawell to move to Denver, and he became chairman and publisher of the *Post*, positions he held until 1981. Seawell was instrumental in the development of the Denver Center for the Performing Arts (DCPA). The Helen G. Bonfils Foundation funded and created a permanent endowment for the DCPA.

Although the newspaper and theater continued to keep her busy, Helen Bonfils's private life in the 1950s and 1960s was marked by poor health and a controversial marriage. Three years after the death of her first husband, the sixty-nine-year-old Bonfils married her twenty-eight-year-old chauffeur "Tiger" Mike Davis. Her health began to fail a few years later, and the second marriage ended in divorce in 1971—amid concern about what her young husband might do with the Bonfils estate. In fact, he received a substantial settlement, including the Bonfils home in east Denver, and used the money to start a successful oil exploration business. By that time Helen Bonfils had little need for the large home, as she was hospitalized much of the time at a suite at St. Joseph's hospital.

The relationship between Helen and her older sister, May, was a rocky one, perhaps aggravated by May's decision to elope in 1904 at the age of twenty-one with a salesman. Fred Bonfils did not approve of the marriage, and nor did fifteen-year-old Helen, who was always her father's favorite. Belle's position has never been indicated. Neither May's eventual divorce from her first husband nor the passage of time did anything to improve the relationship between the three. Indeed, it got worse, and as they grew older the Bonfils sisters eventually stopped speaking to one another. The situation was awkward as both were prominent in Denver society circles, although May lived in a mansion in Lakewood while Helen lived in east Denver. People were careful not to invite them to the same event or party, and May's name was banished from the pages of the *Denver Post*.

After the deaths of her parents, May found that she had been all but cut out of the multi-million-dollar Bonfils estate. She had been left a bequest that provided her with the relatively modest sum of $25,000 a year, while her sister received several million dollars and the Bonfils share of the newspaper. May sued, and eventually received a substantial portion of the estate and a minority allocation of *Post* stock.

Part of her inheritance was a ten-acre piece of land in Lakewood, which she added to over the years and on which she built Belmar, a lavish home modeled after a Versailles palace. It was in 1956 while working on one of her charities, the Central City Opera, that the seventy-three-year-old May Bonfils met and married interior designer Charles Edwin Stanton, who was forty-six. They lived opulently at Belmar, which had by then been expanded to more than 700 acres,

Mary "May" Bonfils Stanton's private mausoleum in the foreground, 100 yards west of the Fairmount Mausoleum where her mother, father, and sister are buried in the Bonfils family vault.

and began planning the sale of some of the land for development of what would become the Belmar residential neighborhood and the downtown center for the City of Lakewood.

In 1960 May sold her *Post* stock to New York publisher Sam Newhouse. She didn't need the money, and observers believed the sale represented just another round in the battle between May and Helen, who was dedicated to keeping control of the newspaper. If her intention was to antagonize her sister, May's sale to Newhouse succeeded. Using May's stock, which represented ownership of 15 percent of the *Post*, Newhouse began a battle to gain control of the paper. The hostile takeover effort lasted twelve bitter years, and although Helen Bonfils's interests eventually prevailed, it was a hollow victory. The *Post* was weakened by the costs and turmoil associated with the Newhouse bid, and also by strong competition from the *News*. As a result, eight years after the victory in the lawsuit, the *Post* was sold to the publisher of the *Los Angeles Times*. In 1980, the Bonfils era at the newspaper came to an end after eighty-five tumultuous years.

Neither Bonfils daughter lived to see the final chapter in the Bonfils–*Post* story. May Bonfils died at her home in 1962 at the age of seventy-eight, and Helen died ten years later at the age of eighty-two. Death alone might have reunited the sisters. But even that final form of reconciliation was not to be. Helen is buried with her mother and father and her first husband, George Somnes, in the Bonfils room in the Fairmount Mausoleum Building, while May is buried outside, a few hundred feet away in a private mausoleum. May's husband, Charles, is buried with his brother Robert in the Fairmount Mausoleum.

One thing both sisters had in common was that they left no heirs. The Fred Bonfils family, if not the name, died with them. As a result, most of their sizeable estates went to charitable purposes, including the DCPA, the University of Colorado Health Sciences Center, various Catholic charities, and many other charities and institutions throughout the state.

$\mathcal{L}$YULPH GILCHRIST STANLEY OGILVY
1861–1947

Colorado's newspapers, like those elsewhere, have had their share of colorful personalities. Yet, perhaps none was more unusual—and certainly none had a longer official title—than Captain the Honorable Lyulph G. S. Ogilvy, DSO. He was the Scottish-born and educated son of an earl, a decorated officer in the British cavalry, and an uncle of Clementine Hozier Churchill, wife of Winston Churchill. Ogilvy enjoyed a long, improbable career as the agricultural writer for the *Denver Post*.

Ogilvy was born in London in 1861. He was a son of the eleventh Earl of Airlie, whose Scottish earldom included thousands of acres and two castles. In Britain first sons were generally amply provided for and traditionally assumed the title and lands of their fathers. Second and subsequent sons, such as Lyulph, were another matter. They usually found a place in the military or the clergy, or, particularly in the last half of the nineteenth century, they were sent to the United States or one of the colonies.

In 1889, when Ogilvy was twenty-eight, his father brought him to Colorado and bought him a 3,500-acre ranch near Greeley, where Crow Creek joins the South Platte River. Despite Ogilvy's best efforts, the ranch failed during the economic depression that followed the financial panic of 1893. It was during this time that Ogilvy began to visit Denver, where he often stayed at one of Denver's best hotels, the Windsor. Ogilvy spent a considerable amount of time in the bar of the Windsor, where he met Buffalo Bill Cody, and where he made

Longtime *Denver Post* agricultural reporter,
L. G. S. Ogilvy, in his customary attire.
COURTESY OF THE COLORADO HISTORICAL SOCIETY, F36890.

what would turn out to be a fortuitous friendship with a bartender named Harry Tammen.

When the ranch failed, Ogilvy turned his attention to war—first as a volunteer in the Spanish-American War in 1898, then as a British cavalry captain in the Boer War in South Africa, where he was wounded in action. Ogilvy, still a British subject, was awarded the Distinguished Service Order by King Edward VII in 1902. Oglivy's father, Earl Ogilvy, also served in the Boer War, where he was killed in action in June 1900 while leading the 12th Lancers Regiment.

After the war, Ogilvy returned to Colorado, and his life underwent a sea change. Before that time he had acquired a reputation as a colorful character, practical joker, and a heavy drinker. His legendary pranks often featured horses, which he loved, and included wild and reckless races across the plains, as well as sneaking the animals into hotels. After a desk clerk at the Windsor Hotel failed to provide a wake-up call, causing Ogilvy to miss an early train, he angrily decided he would take no chances of missing his train the following morning and snuck several roosters into his room. At dawn the flock of roosters did what roosters will do at dawn and woke Ogilvy—and most of the other guests at the hotel. Another time he instigated a chaotic rat hunt at the hotel, emptying a container full of the rodents in the lobby and setting a pack of hunting dogs after them. But his most famous prank was staging his own mock funeral, which included a somber open-casket viewing in downtown Denver and ended at Riverside Cemetery where, with a scotch bottle in hand, he emerged triumphantly from the casket.

That era came to an end in 1902 when Ogilvy bought a small farm near Greeley, married a Loveland woman, also of British descent, and gave up drinking—noting at the time that he felt sure he had consumed enough alcohol in his first forty years to last for the rest of his life.

Ogilvy and his wife, Edith Gertrude Boothroyd, had two children, a daughter, Blanche, who died young, and a son, Jack David Angus Ogilvy, who died in 1993. Jack was on the faculty of the University of Colorado and was a frequent author of articles and features about his father. Edith's poor health eventually forced Ogilvy to sell the farm and move to Denver, where she died in 1908.

By 1909 Ogilvy was nearing middle age and scrambling to make ends meet by working as a night watchman for the Union Pacific railroad. It was at the Denver train station where he and Harry Tammen, who by then was an owner of the *Denver Post,* became reacquainted. Tammen, who also owned a piece of the Sells-Floto circus, was at the station watching the performers and animals boarding a train when he recognized Ogilvy.

One thing led to another, and Tammen, who wanted to attract readers in rural Colorado, offered Ogilvy a job writing about agriculture for the *Post.* Exhibiting the typical Tammen flair for promotion and embellishment, the new reporter was introduced to *Post* readers in 1909 as "Lord" Ogilvy. His fellow workers at the *Post* often called him "Captain." Thus began a memorable career that was to last thirty-six years, with time out for World War I when Ogilvy again responded to the call to arms and served for two years in the British Army.

Ogilvy must have been an odd sight at the *Post*: tall, bearded, dressed in loose-fitting old English suits—pockets stuffed with papers, pencils, pipes, and tobacco—usually wearing a colorful vest and suspenders and often a cap. Nonetheless, he was an excellent writer, knew his subject, and built good relationships with the people who mattered in farming and ranching in Colorado. He fulfilled Tammen's expectations by attracting a wide following among the paper's rural audience.

In 1922 he convinced the *Post* to let him work part time and bought a small ranch near Loveland, where his children were being raised by their maternal grandparents. He continued in this fashion for the next twenty-three years.

When Great Britain went to war against Germany in 1939, the seventy-nine-year-old Ogilvy showed up at a U.S. Army recruiting office, stoop-shouldered and with tobacco streaking his snow-white beard and tried, unsuccessfully, to enlist for what would have been his fourth war. He retired from the *Post* in 1945 and died in Boulder on April 4, 1947, at the age of eighty-five. He is buried at Fairmount Cemetery in Denver, alongside his wife and daughter.

"Lord" Ogilvy's grave at Fairmount Cemetery.

Lawrence Phipps.

Allan Phipps, at left, with his brother **Gerald,** Denver
Broncos General Manager Fred Gehrke, Denver Bears
General Manager Jim Burris, and Rocky Mountain
Empire Sports Board Secretary, Richard S. Kitchen.

ℒAWRENCE COWLE PHIPPS
1862–1958
𝒢ERALD HUGHES PHIPPS
1915–1993
𝒜LLAN ROGERS PHIPPS
1912–1997

In 1901 Lawrence Phipps, a thirty-nine-year-old Pittsburgh millionaire, decided to retire from the steel business in which he had made his fortune and move to what he believed was the healthier climate of Denver. Had Phipps chosen to go elsewhere, many things would have been different for Denver, perhaps most notably that the Denver Broncos would probably be playing their football in Atlanta, and the appearance of the Denver Nuggets, Colorado Avalanche, and Colorado Rockies in Denver might never have occurred at all, and most certainly would have been delayed.

Phipps's road to Denver began in Amwell Township, Pennsylvania, where he was born on August 30, 1862. His father was a Methodist minister. When he was five years old, the family moved to Pittsburgh, which was then already producing over half of the steel and a third of the glass in the United States. Phipps's uncle, Henry, formed a partnership in a small steel foundry with a family friend, Andrew Carnegie. By 1878, Phipps had graduated from high school and joined his uncle working in the steel mill that soon became part of the Carnegie Steel Company.

He was in the right place at the right time. Pittsburgh was one of the nation's fastest growing cities, the vanguard of the rapid industrialization of the nation and led by people with names like Carnegie, Frick, Mellon, Westinghouse, and Heinz. Already rich in coal, the region got an added boost when substantial oil reserves were discovered in the nearby town of Titusville.

When Phipps went to work for Carnegie, the company was just eight years old but was already growing so rapidly that by 1890 it was the largest steel company in the world. During his twenty-six years at Carnegie, Phipps rose from night clerk at $5 a week to vice president and treasurer. In 1901 J. P. Morgan and Henry Frick bought Carnegie Steel and folded it into U.S. Steel. Carnegie walked away with $225 million, worth more than $4.5 billion today. The amount that Phipps received in the buyout was estimated in the press to be $50 million (nearly $500 million today), although the exact amount has never been made public. Phipps was thirty-nine, and decided to retire, or at least to retire from the steel business and from Pennsylvania. He chose Colorado, at least in part because of its reputation as a good place for tuberculosis patients to recover. Phipps did not have the disease, which had killed his mother and his first wife, but his favorite sister, Fanny, did. Fanny, who was helping take care of Phipps's young children, had moved to the state for treatment for tuberculosis and Phipps followed in 1901.

If Phipps had truly intended to retire in Colorado, things didn't work out that way. He invested in and helped run many businesses in the state, including real estate, banking, insurance, and railroads. One of his companies was the Denver and Salt Lake Railroad (or Moffat Road), which—after an infusion of cash from Phipps—survived long enough for the Moffat Tunnel to be completed and for the company to be sold to the Denver and Rio Grande Western. Another Phipps investment was in a large tract of land well south of Denver that by the 1990s became Highlands Ranch, one of the largest and most successful real estate developments in Colorado. In addition, and perhaps taking his cue from Andrew Carnegie, who gave more than half his fortune to charitable causes, Phipps was involved in many philanthropic projects, beginning in 1904 with his giving $11 million to build a tuberculosis sanatorium at Sixth Avenue and Quebec Street, near what is today the Lowry neighborhood, in memory of his mother.

In 1908 Phipps traveled to Wagon Wheel Gap, near Creede, Colorado, for a fishing trip. He liked the area so much that he bought the nearby La Garita Ranch, a 2400-acre property on the Upper Rio Grande River.

Phipps also became increasingly active in Republican Party politics, and in 1918 when he was fifty-six, "Fighting Phipps," as he was described in his campaign flyer, was elected to the United States Senate, narrowly defeating the incumbent, John Shafroth. It was said at the time that he was the Senate's richest member. He served two terms and emerged as a leader in the conservative wing of the Republican Party.

Phipps was married three times. His first wife, Irabella, died in Pennsylvania in 1888. They had a son, Lawrence, Jr., and a daughter, Emma. His second marriage, to attractive eighteen-year-old Genevieve Chandler in 1897, ended in scandal after the second Mrs. Phipps left Denver with the couple's two young daughters and headed for New York. Phipps followed and found her living in a suite at the Waldorf-Astoria Hotel. He took the two young girls and returned to Denver. Charges of kidnapping, negligence, and vague newspaper allusions to Chandler's "men friends," highlighted a highly publicized battle that culminated in the couple's divorce in 1904.

His third marriage was to Margaret Rogers in 1911. She was twenty-six years younger than Phipps and in fact had been a friend of Phipps's twenty-three-year-old daughter Emma. They had two children, Allan and Gerald, and lived on East Colfax at Marion. In 1931, in part to try to generate jobs during that depression year,

Phipps began building an eleven-acre estate at 3400 Belcaro Drive in Denver. The Phipps family gave the property, including its 33,000-square-foot Georgian-style house and a large tennis pavilion, to the University of Denver for use as a conference center. Today it is on the National Register of Historic Places, and is considered to be perhaps the finest example of estate architecture and planning in Colorado. The Phipps family made many other philanthropic gifts, including a donation to the Denver Symphony Orchestra, the Central City Opera, and the Denver Museum of Nature and Science.

In 1950 Phipps and his wife moved to Santa Monica, California, where, although he remained active in Republican politics, he finally managed to retire. He died there on March 1, 1958. The previous year, according to the *Rocky Mountain News*, he had celebrated his ninety-fifth birthday with a cigar, a "highball," and a wish to live to be 100. It was not to be. He was returned to Denver for burial in a family vault in the mausoleum at Fairmount Cemetery. His third wife, Margaret, died in 1968 and is also buried in the family vault. His decision to move to Denver had been a fortuitous one for his adopted state. As legendary *Rocky Mountain News* columnist Lee Casey—no friend of Phipps's politically—wrote: "I cannot think of a single worthy cause to which Senator Phipps has not made a substantial donation. Colorado and Denver are better places because of him. I don't know many of whom that can be said. I wish we could attract more people like that."

Phipps died just two years before the American Football League Denver Broncos' inauspicious arrival in Denver—an event that would be of enormous significance for his sons, Gerald and Allan.

Gerald was born on March 4, 1915, and graduated from Williams College in Massachusetts. He served in the navy in Washington during World War II, then returned to Denver where he entered the construction business, eventually forming Gerald H. Phipps General Contractors in 1952, which is still one of the state's largest construction companies.

One of his early projects was for the minor league Denver Bears baseball team, and Phipps—a sports enthusiast—was persuaded to take stock in the Bears in lieu of payment for some of his work on Bears Stadium (later Mile-High Stadium and since demolished). Then, in 1960, the American Football League was formed, and thanks to the efforts of Larry Varnell, Phipps, and others, Denver was awarded a franchise.

The first years of the Broncos were not only disappointing on the field and at the ticket office, but sartorially as well. The first owners were so poorly financed that they had to buy a drab set of used uniforms, characterized by infamous vertical orange and brown striped socks, which were so ugly that a pair of them is enshrined as a novelty in the Pro Football Hall of Fame. During the Broncos first eight years in existence they won 29, lost 70, and tied 2. Seven of those eight years were losing seasons. In their best year during that stretch, 1962, they struggled to a 7–7 record, only to have any hopes of improvement dashed when they began the next season with a 59–7 loss to Kansas City, following which they completed the season with a record of two wins, eleven losses, and a tie.

Even before the first losing season was completed, the franchise was rumored to be on its way to San Antonio. Gerald and Allan Phipps and a local group stepped forward and bought a minority interest, temporarily saving the team. The old uniforms—which Gerald Phipps particularly hated—were burned in a public ceremony. But it didn't make any difference. Three years later, and following their two consecutive 2–11–1 seasons and millions of dollars in losses, the majority owners wanted out, and voted to sell the franchise to Cox Broadcasting, which planned to move the team to its headquarters in Atlanta. Cox, however, didn't want any minority owners such as the Phipps muddying the water, and they refused to join the deal. Instead, the Phipps brothers stepped up again—this time with an offer to buy out the majority owners for $1.5 million.

After several days of frantic negotiations, the deal was done, and the Broncos stayed put.

At the time the sale was announced, a reporter reflected on the team's dismal history of turmoil and losing money and asked Gerald Phipps why he had agreed to the deal. Phipps was quiet and thoughtful for a few moments, before replying, "Sometimes I think I'm a stupid idiot."

His decision was a good one. From that point on, the Broncos became an object of civic pride and a financial success, selling more than 22,000 season tickets in 1965—almost three times the number sold the previous year. There remained a few small problems, including a threat by the league to move the team to Birmingham in 1967 if the stadium wasn't expanded and the continued dismal on-field performance—the Broncos didn't achieve a winning season until 1973, their fourteenth year! But by then Denver had emphatically adopted the Broncos, and although the Phipps sold their interest in the team in 1981 for a reported $40 million, the team had long since achieved respectability, including reaching the Super Bowl for the first time in 1977.

In 1985 Gerald Phipps was the first non-player to be inducted into the Denver Broncos "Ring of Fame."

He was married twice: to Janet Alice Smith, who died in 1988, and then to Muriel Stokes Magarrell in 1989. He died at home in Denver on August 6, 1993, at the age of seventy-eight, and his ashes are interred at All Souls Walk at St. John's Episcopal Cathedral in Denver.

Allan Phipps was born in Denver on October 3, 1912. In school he was an outstanding student and athlete, being named to the Phi Beta Kappa honor society in his junior year at Williams, and also lettering on the tennis and swimming teams.

He went on to receive law degrees from the University of Denver and Oxford University. It was while he was in England in

The Phipps's vault in Fairmount Mausoleum, where Lawrence Phipps is entombed.

Gerald Phipps's ashes are interred in this area of All Soul's Walk, at St. John's Episcopal Cathedral in Denver.

The Phipps family's La Garita Ranch near Creede, where Allan Phipps's ashes were scattered.

PHOTO COURTESY OF PAUL PRENTISS AND FRONT RANGE ANGLERS.

1936 that he met and married his first wife, Doreen Evans, a twenty-year-old race-car driver. The couple moved to Denver in 1938 and built their home at 885 South Garfield Street. Phipps became a member of the Colorado bar in 1938 and began practicing law, which was interrupted when he served as a lieutenant commander on carriers in the Far East during World War II. He returned to Denver in 1946 to join the law firm of Hughes and Dorsey. In 1953 Phipps's marriage to his first wife ended in divorce, and in 1955 he married Clara Mitchell Van Schaack.

Phipps was an active outdoorsman, enjoying hunting, fishing, and skiing—and was one of the founders of the Winter Park ski area. He was inducted into the Colorado Ski Hall of Fame in 1988 and was named Colorado philanthropist of the year in 1991. Although less publicly associated with the Broncos than his brother Gerald, Allan was a co-owner and served as president of the organization while Gerald was chairman.

He died on September 15, 1997 at the age of eighty-four in Denver. His funeral service was held at St. John's Cathedral and his ashes were dispersed at the family's La Garita Ranch in southwestern Colorado.

Allan and Gerald Phipps, like their father, were successful in their careers and as philanthropists, but they will always be remembered best as "the people who saved the Broncos," and helped put Denver on the map in major league sports.

$\mathcal{S}$PENCER PENROSE
1865–1939

Two of Colorado's most famous and enduringly popular hotels had their beginnings at the same time—the early 1890s. But while Denver's Brown Palace was a luxury hotel from the beginning, The Broadmoor in Colorado Springs began its existence in 1891 as a small and undistinguished hotel adjacent to a casino and surrounded by a 2,400-acre land development. Over the next twenty years the hotel failed to prosper. By 1914 it had been turned into a girl's boarding school and might never have become what it is today had it not attracted the attention of fifty-three-year-old Spencer Penrose, who had made a fortune in mining and real estate in the mountains west of Colorado Springs.

Penrose was born in 1865 in Philadelphia, one of six brothers in a prominent and wealthy family. An older brother, Boise, became a United States senator and Republican Party leader, and is credited with having coined the phrase "public office is the last refuge of a scoundrel." His other brothers also established successful and traditional careers but, following his graduation from Harvard in 1886, Spencer Penrose turned down an offer of a job in a bank and headed West with no clear idea of what the future had in store for him.

Having heard stories of gold strikes south of the border, Penrose headed first for Mexico, then worked his way north to Las Cruces, New Mexico. He was living there in 1891 when he was invited to visit Colorado Springs by a friend from Philadelphia, Charles L. Tutt. While Penrose was visiting Tutt, news came that a major gold find had

Spencer Penrose, at left, with his
partner Charles Tutt in the early days.

The Will Rogers Shrine of the Sun, Colorado Springs.
Burial site of Spencer and Julie Penrose.

occurred at Cripple Creek in the mountains west of Colorado Springs.

Penrose headed to Cripple Creek, where by 1894 he had made a fortune in mining, real estate, and ore processing, often in partnership with Tutt. Among the many successful Penrose ventures was a small Utah copper company which he acquired for pennies a share and that subsequently became part of Kennecott Copper, one of the world's largest copper mining companies. It is now part of Rio Tinto PLC, a $38 billion international mining company with headquarters in London and Melbourne. Penrose's career was notably not all work and no play. Cripple Creek was a wide-open and bustling town in those days, with a population of more than 20,000, and the handsome and wealthy "Spec" Penrose enjoyed it to the fullest. He acquired a reputation for seldom arising before noon and seldom getting home before dawn. Fortunately for him the venue for doing business in the 1890s in Cripple Creek was not the office or the boardroom, but the saloon, and deals were made over drinks, not spreadsheets.

By the early 1900s the boom in Cripple Creek had slowed, and Penrose began spending most of his time in Colorado Springs and Europe, where, in London in 1906, he married Detroit-born Julie Villiers McMillan. She originally had moved to Colorado Springs with her first husband, a wealthy Michigan man who died of tuberculosis in 1902. In 1909 Penrose's partner, Tutt, died of a heart attack while he was in New York, and Penrose became guardian for his young son Charles Tutt, Jr.

Penrose was one of the few who not only made a fortune in mining, but also managed to keep it. While mining opportunities were disappearing, he diversified into other businesses, and his El Pomar Investment Company owned interests in railroads, ranching, banking, tourism, and hotel operations.

The idea of building an elegant resort hotel intrigued Penrose, as a result of his many trips to Europe, where he stayed in the best spas and resorts and developed an appreciation of art and architecture—

perhaps a remnant of a childhood desire to be an artist. He was convinced of Colorado Springs' attractiveness as a tourist destination, and in 1915 he financed the construction of the Pikes Peak Highway.

In 1916 Penrose moved to his El Pomar estate, which was south of downtown Colorado Springs and adjacent to the original Broadmoor hotel property. The hotel had endured several lean years and Penrose was able to buy the 450 acres for $90,000 in 1917. He hired a New York firm, Warren and Wetmore, to design the new hotel, and Charles Tutt, Jr., to oversee the construction. The hotel opened in the summer of 1918, following just thirteen months of rapid and expensive construction.

The Broadmoor was successful from the start, helped by Penrose's own abilities as a promoter. In 1920, for example, he helped put the Broadmoor on the map by hosting a week-long "Arabian Nights Party," which was said to have been the costliest hotel promotion ever held. Penrose invited fifty of the most prominent hotel and travel executives to be his guests at the Broadmoor. He arranged for their transportation in two well-provisioned private railway cars: the *Newport* and the *Mather*, aboard *The Broadmoor Special,* courtesy of the New York Central and the Rock Island Railroad. Throughout the Roaring Twenties the Broadmoor attracted much publicity and many celebrities, including heavyweight boxing champion Jack Dempsey, who used the Broadmoor as his training site.

Celebrities, along with many others, were attracted by the beauty of the hotel and by golf, polo and—during a time when prohibition was the law of the land—Penrose's fabled private hoard of wines and liquors. These were often available for privileged guests at The Cooking Club, a small social organization founded by Penrose and some of his old friends. It was one of scores of private clubs throughout the world to which Penrose belonged.

Prohibition also marked the only time that Penrose strayed from the Republican Party, where he was an influential leader. In the 1928 presidential race he supported New York Governor Al Smith, a Democrat but also a Catholic and, reportedly, a man who enjoyed drinking alcohol on occasion and was someone who would fight for repeal of prohibition. Smith lost, prohibition remained until the first term of Franklin D. Roosevelt, and Penrose returned to the Republican fold. He often said that Roosevelt's willingness to be rid of prohibition was the only issue on which he agreed with FDR.

By the 1930s, the Penroses began spending more time traveling and the responsibility of managing the Penrose interests fell more and more to Charles Tutt and his sons, Thayer and Russell. While the hotel had done well during the 1920s, like most businesses it was weakened by the Great Depression and had to go through bankruptcy reorganization in 1932.

By 1937, the hotel was again prospering, but Penrose's health was failing. He had been diagnosed with throat cancer several years earlier, and at the age of seventy-two he realized he might not have long to live. He and his wife, who had inherited a substantial sum of money from her first husband, established the El Pomar Foundation, which provided funding for a variety of charitable, health-care, and educational organizations.

He also built the Shrine of the Sun on Cheyenne Mountain, which was dedicated to Will Rogers, a popular and much-beloved entertainer who had died in an airplane accident in 1935. Interestingly, Penrose scarcely knew Rogers and had originally intended that the shrine be in his own honor, but his wife convinced him that such a monumental project would be in bad taste—too immodest, even for him. At about the same time he decided to give the Cheyenne Mountain Zoo, which he originally built near the Broadmoor for guests of the hotel, to the City of Colorado Springs, for which it became the municipal zoo.

In 1939 Penrose traveled abroad one more time before returning to Colorado Springs, where he dedicated a new rodeo arena just west of the hotel and announced a large contribution to a cancer research center in Colorado Springs.

He died on December 7, 1939, at home, at the age of seventy-four, and his ashes were interred in a private ceremony at the Shrine of the Sun. Colorado has had many successful entrepreneurs, but probably none who enjoyed his life and his money more than Penrose, or who lived with such confidence and style.

Penrose's wife, who served as president of the El Pomar Foundation, died in 1956 at the age of eighty-five. After her husband's death she donated their El Pomar home to the Sisters of Charity. She lived the rest of her life first in an apartment at the Broadmoor and then, from 1954 to 1956, in a small house on Cheyenne Mountain near her husband's Cooking Club. She, too, was interred at the Shrine of the Sun.

Under the management of Russell and Thayer Tutt, the Broadmoor continued to grow and prosper as an asset of the El Pomar Foundation until 1988, when changes in tax laws governing such organizations led the foundation to sell a majority interest in the property and some other Penrose ventures. The buyer was the Oklahoma Publishing Company, headed by Edward L. Gaylord, who had attended Colorado College and whose company owned a Colorado Springs newspaper.

There is scarcely any aspect of life in and around Colorado Springs that has not been profoundly affected by the decision of Spencer Penrose to visit his friend Charles Tutt in Colorado Springs in 1891. The Broadmoor continues to be one of the most distinctive and successful resorts in the world, and since Penrose and his wife had no children of their own the bulk of their fortune has gone back into the community. Their El Pomar Foundation, whose assets have grown from $21 million to over $475 million, is the third largest foundation in Colorado. Its annual gifts now exceed $22 million and are given primarily to Colorado recipients.

WILLIAM STERNE FRIEDMAN
1868–1944

Denver's Congregation Emanuel was the first Jewish house of worship in Denver. During the course of its history Temple Emanuel evolved from a small congregation to the Rocky Mountain's largest, from a theologically traditional congregation to a Reform one, and from a relatively passive and closed organization to an activist and inclusive one. Congregation Emanuel's growth and character are largely the result of the efforts of William S. Friedman, rabbi from 1889 to 1938.

Friedman was born in Chicago on October 24, 1868, but grew up in Cincinnati, where he received both his college degree from the University of Cincinnati and, in 1889, his rabbinical degree from Hebrew Union College. Immediately after graduation he received an offer to come to Denver as a rabbi at Congregation Emanuel, which at the time of his arrival in August 1889, was a small, struggling temple with fewer than fifty families.

Friedman brought to his position a concept of the role of a rabbi, and indeed of a temple or a religion itself, which was relatively new in the United States, and decidedly so for a Jewish congregation in the West. When Friedman arrived in Denver he found a community in which most Jews worshiped quietly, even covertly, preferring to keep their faith separate from the other parts of their lives. It was partly a matter of tradition, but also reflected a desire to blend in and avoid attracting attention. Jews, along with other minorities, suffered from discrimination and prejudice.

Rabbi William Friedman.
COURTESY OF THE CONGREGATION TEMPLE EMANUEL.

Rabbi Friedman's gravesite in the Emanuel
section of Fairmount Cemetery.

Friedman saw things differently. Over the course of his nearly half-century as rabbi of Congregation Emanuel, he became an outspoken and effective community leader. His example paved the way for others such as Charles E. Hillel Kauvar, who became rabbi at Beth Hamedrosh Hagadol thirteen years after Friedman took over at Emanuel.

While some of Friedman's efforts were directed toward fighting anti-Semitism, his passion in life was working for the benefit of all people. He reached out from the Temple and forged spiritual and practical ties with Denver's other religions. He established a practice—which continues to this day—of having leaders of those religions bring their messages to the congregation at Emanuel; and he visited their places of worship. Rabbi Friedman viewed Judaism as a "religion of humanity," and but one part of a larger religious mosaic, a grouping of equals. He was mistrustful of Zionism and of those he saw as over-zealous traditionalists. He challenged those who demanded a Jewish homeland, and urged American Jews to think of America as their permanent home, rather than a Jewish state in Palestine. "Judaism," he wrote, "needs no particular land any more than . . . any other religion. Our message is not national nor political, but spiritual." However, it is important to note that Friedman's views on this subject predated the Holocaust, although he had visited Europe in the 1930s and spoke out against Nazi persecution of Jews and others.

Rabbi Friedman was not reluctant to take the lead in social and community causes. Shortly after he arrived in Denver, he helped lead the effort started by Frances Wisebart Jacobs to found a hospital to serve the many people who were flocking to Colorado's climate because of tuberculosis and other respiratory problems. In 1899, thanks to the efforts of Friedman and the Jewish community, the National Jewish Medical and Research Center opened the doors of its first structure: the William S. Friedman Building. It was the first such hospital in the country that offered free medical care to indigent tuberculosis patients.

Another Friedman project was Denver's Charity Organization Society, a non-sectarian welfare and charitable services provider that was started in 1887. When Friedman arrived in Denver he became a leader of the charity, along with other religious leaders including the Reverend Myron W. Reed of the First Congregational Church, Monsignor William J. O'Ryan of St. Leo the Great Catholic Church, and Reverend H. Martyn Hart of St. John's Episcopal Cathedral. Friedman was vice president of the organization from 1890 to 1901 and president of the Colorado Board of Charities and Corrections from 1904 to 1910. The Charity Organization Society was so successful that it was the model for what later became the United Way.

Although he received offers to move to larger congregations in cities such as New York and San Francisco, Friedman remained at Congregation Emanuel, where he had been elected "Rabbi for life" in 1919. During his tenure the congregation moved from a small building at Twenty-Fourth and Curtis Streets to new facilities at Sixteenth Avenue and Pearl Street, and eventually became the largest Jewish congregation in the region, now located at First Avenue and Forest Street.

In the spring of 1938, at the age of seventy, he suffered a stroke while playing golf. He never regained enough strength to resume his duties at Congregation Emanuel and in 1939 moved to California where he lived in retirement with his wife, Juliet, and their daughter. Following his death in Coronado Beach in April 1944, his body was returned to Denver for services at Congregation Emanuel and burial in the Emanuel section of Fairmount Cemetery. His wife died in California in 1956 and is also buried at Fairmount.

Friedman's greatest legacy is certainly Congregation Emanuel itself—with a membership numbering in thousands and a continuing tradition of involvement in social issues in the community.

*E*MILY GRIFFITH
1868–1947

Emily Griffith was born in Cincinnati in 1868. Her family moved to Nebraska, where she became a teacher by accident. In 1881, while she was a student in a small, sod schoolhouse near Broken Bow, Nebraska, the woman who was teaching the class left to get married. There was no one else available. Emily, age thirteen, took over and began teaching eight grades in one room. The following year, her interim status was made official when she passed the teachers' examination. After moving to Denver in 1895, she worked in the Twenty-Fourth Street School in Five Points, at that time one of Denver's lowest income neighborhoods.

From teaching the poor and disadvantaged among Denver's children, Griffith became aware that the needs of many students were not being met by the existing system of education. In addition, she got to know the parents of her students and found that many of them lacked the necessary skills to support themselves financially and create good homes for their children. Griffith started tutoring some of these parents, and she began to understand their need for a more basic and flexible kind of education than was then available. She became a crusader for a new curriculum designed to meet the needs of people, especially young adults, who were unable to adapt to traditional classroom teaching and schedules. Griffith lobbied for her ideas, and gradually secured the support of the school board and influential members of the community, including the *Denver Post,* which editorialized in favor of Griffith's plan. As a result, in 1916

Emily Griffith, founder of the Opportunity School.
COURTESY OF DENVER PUBLIC SCHOOLS.

Gravesite of Emily Griffith and her sister Florence at Fairmount Cemetery.

Denver Public Schools created the Opportunity School at Fourteenth and Welton Streets in downtown Denver. Initially, Griffith, the principal, was given five teachers and two classrooms in the old Longfellow school building, which had been condemned. The school offered day and night classes for adults needing basic skills including math and English as well as practical trades such as electronics, auto mechanics, and typing. Recognizing that many of her students lacked money for food, Emily and her sister Florence also began serving students free soup at the school.

The impact of the Opportunity School cannot be overestimated. It was immediately successful. Expecting just a handful of students would enroll and occupy the two classrooms, school officials were astounded when more than 1,400 students signed up the first week the school was open. Since its opening, it has admitted over 1.3 million students, including immigrants for whom the school was a first chance to learn how to make their way in a new country, and people who had dropped out of traditional schools. For many of them, Opportunity School was the last chance they would have to gain an education.

When the United States entered the World Wars, the school shifted its emphasis to training for defense industries, and during World War II the school was open around the clock.

The school Emily Griffith created became famous internationally and provided the model for similar schools elsewhere. While she had never attended college, Griffith received an honorary master of education degree from the University of Colorado and was president of the Colorado Education Association. Her significance to Colorado is memorialized by her portrait in a stained glass window at the state capitol.

In 1933 Griffith retired as principal, and the school was renamed the Emily Griffith Opportunity School. Thereafter she lived on a small pension, taking care of her sister Florence, whose health was poor. Although there had been several suitors in her life, Emily Griffith never married.

Instead she and Florence moved to a small summer-type cabin in Pinecliffe in the mountains west of Boulder, where they lived year-round. The cabin had been built by a long-time close Griffith friend and fellow teacher, Fred Lundy, who eventually moved nearby where he could help look after the sisters.

Early on June 20, 1947, Emily's youngest sister, Ethel, went to the cabin to visit Florence and Emily, who was then seventy-nine. Ethel had stopped by the day before, but there had been no answer to her knock, and no sign of her sisters. This time she brought a key. When she and her husband entered the cabin they found both women dead in their bedrooms, shot in the backs of their heads.

Ethel and her husband went to Lundy's house for help, but he was gone. His car was later found abandoned, and his body was recovered from nearby South Boulder Creek. In the car was a letter containing burial instructions, and on the seat of the car was a .38 revolver, which proved to be the weapon that had fired the shots that killed the Griffith sisters. The case was never officially solved. Speculation included a mercy killing or a possible suicide pact between the three, who were all elderly and in failing health.

Griffith's legacy lives on, however, and today the school occupies an entire block in downtown Denver, with satellite facilities—including an aircraft-training center—in other locations. With more than 14,500 students and 350 instructors, the school offers many degree and apprentice programs and hundreds of courses in everything from cake decorating to computer technology.

Emily Griffith and her sister are buried at Fairmount Cemetery.

$\mathcal{J}$USTINA L. FORD
1871–1952

Justina Laurena Ford, the first African-American woman doctor licensed to practice medicine in Colorado—and one of the first in the nation—was born on January 22, 1871, in Knoxville, Illinois, and grew up in nearby Galesburg, where her mother was a nurse. She received her medical education at Hering Medical College in Chicago, and began working as a physician in 1900 in Normal, Alabama, with a practice specializing in gynecology, obstetrics, and pediatrics.

It was not an easy career, beginning as it did at a time when only a handful of women were doctors, and very few of them were African-American. Meeting resistance to her practice in Alabama, where she was the first African-American woman to try to practice medicine, Ford decided to move to Denver in 1902, a city which, she felt, had a more open attitude about racial matters than most other cities. She hung out her shingle at her 2334 Arapahoe Street home.

Colorado may have been a better place than Alabama for an African-American doctor to practice, but it was hardly ideal. In the early 1900s the Colorado Medical Society did not admit African-Americans, a restriction that prevented Ford, and the five male African-American doctors who were practicing in Denver at the time, from becoming members of the American Medical Association. This, in turn, prevented their accreditation at Denver hospitals. Indeed, not only did hospitals in Colorado not accept

Dr. Justina Ford, with her nephew.
COURTESY OF THE DENVER PUBLIC LIBRARY,
WESTERN HISTORY COLLECTION, Z8947.

Justina Ford's gravesite at Fairmount Cemetery.

African-American doctors, some would not even admit African-American or other minority patients.

Most of her patients were recent immigrants and minorities—not only African-Americans but also Asians, Mexicans, and Greeks. Indeed, by the time of her death she was able to converse with patients in seven languages. However, being unable to use some hospitals was not as big a problem as might have been the case had Ford's specialty not been obstetrics. For much of the first half of the twentieth century it was common for births to take place at home. And, if some hospitals didn't want immigrants and minorities it was fine with many of them, who often distrusted the medical establishment and had strong traditions of home childbirth. Ford was able to carry out a significant part of her practice in her patients' homes or at her office. She was a believer in natural childbirth, and—in so far as possible—in natural forms of medicine. Hering Medical College, from which she was graduated, included homeopathy in its curriculum, and turned out many doctors who practiced homeopathic medicine.

During the course of her fifty-year career in Denver, she is estimated to have delivered more than 5,000, and perhaps as many as 7,000, babies. She had a reputation as the "Lady Doctor" who would turn away no patient. She often received little or no cash fee for her services, and it was not unusual for her patients to pay their bills in goods and services. There are also many stories of Ford not only providing medical care, but also assisting her patients and their families by providing them with food, blankets, and coal.

Although she was losing her eyesight, Ford continued her practice right up to the end, which came on October 14, 1952, when she died at home at the age of eighty-one. She was buried at Fairmount Cemetery.

In the course of her career her example served to begin to reduce or eliminate some of the obstacles facing minorities in Colorado. As she once said, she "fought like a tiger against the barriers of race and sex." Although eventually she was admitted to practice at Denver General Hospital, in some ways the situation at the end of her career was not much improved. As the *Denver Inquirer* noted in its 1952 obituary, fifty years after her arrival in Denver, she was still Colorado's "first and only Negro woman M.D."

She was married twice: first to a clergyman named Ford, whose name she took and, following his death, to Alfred Allen, who survived her.

In 1989, the Colorado Medical Society honored her "as an outstanding figure in the development and furtherance of health care in Colorado." She is in the Colorado Women's Hall of Fame, and a Justina Ford Medical Society was established at the University of Colorado Health Sciences Center. Her memory also lives on through the Ford-Warren Public Library and the Black American West Museum and Heritage Center, which is located in her former Arapahoe Street home. The home, which was built in 1889, had been scheduled for demolition in 1983 to make way for a parking lot, but was saved through efforts of Historic Denver and local companies. In 1984 the nine-room, Victorian-style building was moved to its present location at 3091 California Street, and is on the National Register of Historical Landmarks.

A bronze statue of Ford, holding a newborn child, was commissioned by the Regional Transportation District and stands at the light rail station that is across the street from the Museum. It was designed by local artist Jess DuBois, who grew up in Ford's Five Points neighborhood and knew many people who had been delivered by her. When her statue was dedicated in 1998, DuBois spoke with a *Denver Post* reporter and summed up Ford's career: "When I was young, I couldn't figure out why the Lady Doctor would stay here with us when she could . . . make more money. But now I hold to the belief that she was truly God-sent. There were so many people that couldn't afford doctors, and she was the only doctor in the area."

WILLIAM MACLEOD RAINE
1871–1954

Today, the Western novels of Denver author Bill
Raine are no longer in print, and Westerns themselves are seldom
found on the bestseller lists. However, in the first half of the twentieth century, the Western novel tradition was robust, and authors
such as Zane Grey, Max Brand, Owen Wister, and William MacLeod
Raine were among the leading Western writers. In his long lifetime,
Raine wrote eighty books, several of which were made into movies
as well as hundreds of short stories and magazine articles. By the
1930s, Raine's books, including such titles as *The Trail of Danger* and
The Knife Through the Ace, were bestsellers in both the United States
and England and were translated into many other languages.

Raine was an unlikely prospect to become a Western author. He
was born in London, England, on June 22, 1871, son of a Scottish
merchant. It is likely he would have spent most of his life in England
had it not been for his mother's unexpected death at a young age—
an event which devastated his father. At loose ends, the elder Raine
became intrigued by advertisements that were beginning to appear
proclaiming the attractions of frontier life in the United States. At
the age of ten, Raine, his three brothers, and his father moved to
Arkansas and bought land to grow fruit and raise cattle.
Unfortunately, Raine's health was poor, and he was unable to participate in much riding and ranching—but he watched and learned,
getting to know the land, the cattle business, and the characters who
made their livings on the frontier.

Author **"Wild Bill" Raine** at his desk. The shoes are
a clue that Raine was more city slicker than cowboy.
COURTESY OF THE DENVER PUBLIC LIBRARY,
WESTERN HISTORY COLLECTION, Z1973.

Bill Raine's grave at Fairmount Cemetery.

When he was eighteen he left the ranch in Arkansas, and enrolled at Oberlin College in Ohio. There he began to write, first as a sportswriter for the local newspaper and then as a stringer for the *Chicago Tribune* and the *Cincinnati Inquirer.* He did well at Oberlin and remained active and involved with the school for the rest of his life.

Following Raine's graduation in 1894 he headed West to be near his father, who had bought a farm near Seattle. Raine was still too sickly to be of much help in farm activities—his illness had been diagnosed as tuberculosis—and he turned to less strenuous pursuits, first as a teacher and then as a reporter for the *Seattle Times.*

Despite his poor health, when the Spanish–American War broke out in 1898, Raine tried to enlist. He was told that not only was he too ill to be accepted into the army, but also that his life would be in danger if he did not go to Colorado, which offered the preferred climate at that time for those suffering from tuberculosis. Raine took the advice and joined the thousands of TB sufferers for whom Colorado seemed the only chance—in those pre-antibiotic days— for leading a healthy life.

In Denver, Raine continued working as a newspaper reporter but also began having success writing adventure fiction, mostly romantic period pieces based on English history, for national magazines. His health improved sufficiently for him to travel throughout the West, and his fiction began to reflect these experiences and the lives of the cowboys and other people he met, including lawmen and outlaws such as Bat Masterson, John Wesley Hardin, and Wyatt Earp.

In 1905 he married Jennie Langley, and in 1906 his first full-length Western novel, *Wyoming: A Story of the Outdoor West,* was published—and his fifty-year career as a successful Western author was underway. Published first by Doubleday, then by Houghton Mifflin, Raine's books sold over 15 million copies. Although his writing was always full of action, it also reflected his scholarly interest in the

West, and most of his books contain real characters and settings from Western history. He also wrote several well-received Western non-fiction books, including *Famous Sheriffs and Western Outlaws.* His success was reflected in his earnings, which averaged more than $25,000 annually for more than three decades. In 1923 he reported earning $150,000; this was approximately what heads of major corporations were earning, twice the salary of the President of the United States, and three times what Babe Ruth earned while leading the Major Leagues with forty-one home runs.

Raine's first wife Jennie died in 1920, and in 1924 he married Florence Hollingsworth. They lived at 150 Race Street in Denver's Country Club neighborhood. During those years he found time to do other work, including occasional newspaper writing. He was a close friend of Lee Casey, the well-respected editor of the *Rocky Mountain News.* In Raine's obituary in the *News*, the story was told of the time when Casey convinced Raine, who had helped create the journalism school at the University of Colorado, to run for the job of regent on the school's governing body. In the course of the campaign a short autobiography was needed for some campaign literature. Raine, whose nickname was "Wild Bill"—a reference to his "rip-snorting" Western writing more than to his personality, which was quiet and modest—couldn't resist the temptation and penned a colorful and fictional account of his life. It told of arriving in Denver "a jump ahead of the sheriff" and completing his education "by drawing to inside straights at the Press Club." Raine apparently believed his biographical sketch would just be a joke between himself, Casey, and a few friends, but opposition Republican newspapers got hold of it and printed it. Raine was the only Democrat on the ballot to lose in 1932—the year of the Roosevelt landslide.

Failure at politics had no ill effect on Raine's writing career. The 1930s were one of his most successful and prolific periods, during which he published more than fifteen novels, several of them appearing on bestseller lists.

In 1942 Raine's second wife died, and three years later—at the age of seventy-four—he married Claire Parmeley. They lived at 1200 East Third Avenue and, later, at 601 Franklin Street. Raine gradually cut back on his writing in the last ten years of his life, although he still tried to produce at least 500 words a day—down from over a thousand in his younger years. However, he still enjoyed such a strong reputation that in the late 1940s the Stetson Hat Company brought out a new ten-gallon cowboy hat named the *Bill Raine,* which he dutifully wore for the opening ceremony of the National Western Stock Show and Rodeo. He was also named honorary president of the Western Writers of America organization in 1954.

Raine died on July 25, 1954, at the age of eighty-three, just one week after a story about him and his latest novel, *Reluctant Gunman,* appeared in *Time* magazine. In the two years following his death two movies appeared which were based on his work: *The Man from Bitter Ridge* (1955) starring Lex Barker, and *Three Young Texans* (1954) starring Jeffrey Hunter. A bit player in *Texans* was twenty-nine-year-old Aaron Spelling, a struggling performer whose acting career never took off, but who later achieved fame and fortune as the television producer of such shows as *Charlie's Angels* and *The Love Boat.* The novel Raine had been working on at the time of his death, *High Grass Valley,* was published in 1955 after it was completed by Raine's friend Wayne D. Overholser, another award-winning Western author. Another novel, *The Young Tenderfoot,* was found after his death and published posthumously in 1958. The following year he was elected to the National Cowboy Hall of Fame.

Raine is buried at Fairmount Cemetery.

Dr. John Locke in 1918, three years before he became the grand dragon of Colorado's Ku Klux Klan.
COURTESY OF THE COLORADO HISTORICAL SOCIETY, F6316.

Dr. John Locke's mausoleum at Fairmount Cemetery.

$\mathcal{J}$OHN GALEN LOCKE
1873–1935

During the 1920s the Ku Klux Klan enjoyed a brief, yet destructive, reign in Colorado. Indeed, the Klan was probably as influential in Colorado as it was anywhere, and there was not a branch of government untouched by sympathizers. The leader of the movement was a complex and enigmatic Denver doctor who exerted the kind of power that is generally associated with political "bosses" such William M. Tweed in New York or Tom Pendergast in Kansas City.

John Galen Locke was born in 1873 in Port Henry, New York. He and his wife, Tessie, moved to Colorado in 1893. Locke served in the Philippines during the Spanish–American War and returned to Denver where, in 1904, he received a degree from the Denver Homeopathic College and set up a practice with his father at 1345 Glenarm Place in downtown Denver.

Locke's practice was reasonably successful, if unorthodox. He favored homeopathy and was not popular with the city's traditional medical establishment. His physical appearance was bizarre: he was short and quite overweight, had a moustache and goatee, and was often accompanied by three large dogs. Initially, there was little evidence in his lifestyle to suggest that he was likely to become a Klan member, let alone a "grand dragon." His political views seemed mainstream. He was a Democrat and a member of such organizations as the Lakewood Country Club, the Denver Athletic Club, and the Episcopal Church. His hobbies included riding and hunting. Locke and his wife had one child, a son who died at age seven. The Lockes were divorced in 1906, remarried in 1912, and separated again in 1918.

The original Ku Klux Klan had arisen out of the ashes of the Civil War as a white supremacist organization founded by former Confederate soldiers, but it had all but disappeared by 1880. A new Klan, which was started in Georgia in 1915, was still anti-Black, but it was also anti-Catholic, anti-foreign, anti-communist, and anti-Semitic. It was super-patriotic, pro-law-and-order, and pro-religion—at least fundamental Protestantism. This new Klan was a national, not Southern, phenomenon, and in addition to Colorado it elected public officials in states from Oregon to Maine. Many of the Klan's basic beliefs were shared by political leaders such as presidents Theodore Roosevelt and Woodrow Wilson, as well as by federal judges—including a justice of the Supreme Court—and members of Congress. It was even claimed, but never proven, that Warren Harding, president from 1920–23, was a Klan member.

By 1922, five million Americans, and 50,000 Coloradans, were active Klan members. John Locke had been recruited by Klan leaders in 1921, and quickly became the leader, or grand dragon, of the Klan in the state, with headquarters in the fortified basement of his medical office.

Locke was an unusual Klan leader in at least one respect: while he paid lip service to the Klan's policies, he showed little personal animosity toward minorities and no enthusiasm for violence. In 1924, for example, Locke intervened forcefully to prevent a Klan-inspired gang from burning a Catholic cathedral. Locke also employed Catholics—in defiance of national Klan policy—and one contemporary news story claimed that Locke's wife was Catholic. Sensing that the Klan's rhetoric was not always a reflection of Locke himself, several Catholic leaders in Colorado became friends with Locke, and one priest was an honorary pallbearer at Locke's funeral.

Rather than being motivated by bigotry, hatred, or ideology, Locke's reason for joining the Klan appears to have been simply to wield power. He viewed the Klan opportunistically as an emerging political force that he could dominate. Locke's management of the "Kolorado Klan" was generally shrewd, and he proved to be a skillful organizer. He sensed that for the Klan to grow, it would have to link itself more with popular causes than with cross-burnings and bombings—although those did occur. Under Locke's leadership the Klan came to be associated with seemingly benevolent gestures and popular issues such as tough law-enforcement and clean government.

In the early 1920s, Denver was a city with a rising crime rate, characterized by rampant bootlegging, gambling, and prostitution. The government and police force were seen as ineffective at best, corrupt at worst. The Klan jumped on these crime problems and then used them to justify its attacks on "Italian bootleggers" and "Jewish gamblers."

Locke's first political opportunity came in 1923, when the Klan supported Ben Stapleton in the Denver mayoral election. Following the election, Stapleton in turn appointed Klan members to key positions, including chief of police and city attorney. On at least one occasion the city auditorium was used for a Klan meeting.

By 1924, Klansmen were in office throughout the state and the Klan was nearing the peak of its power. Locke and the Klan worked hard in the 1924 general election, and by the time the dust had settled on election day the Klan controlled both the state of Colorado and the city of Denver. Once again the Klan had skillfully hidden behind a popular movement: the national Republican ticket of Calvin Coolidge. The Klan's slate was elected, including a close Locke associate as governor and another Klan member in the United States Senate. Klansmen also gained a majority in the state legislature.

However, 1924 actually marked the high point of the Klan. Its attempts to govern and to pass the Klan agenda were largely unsuccessful, and a recall effort against Stapleton was narrowly defeated only after the expenditure of a large amount of Klan funds. In 1925 Locke was charged with tax evasion, and briefly jailed. Although he was exonerated, the effect of the charge was damaging. The Klan's empire began to crumble. The press attacked Locke, and a coalition of legislators managed to block Klan legislation. Mayor Stapleton, reacting to allegations of corruption in the police department, fired the Klansman police chief. Even the national Klan organization broke with Locke, forcing him to resign.

Locke tried to rally, founding "Minute Men of America," whose uniforms were copies of those worn by troops during the American Revolution. A few thousand people followed Locke, but most Klansmen drifted away. By 1930 national Klan membership had fallen to fewer than 30,000 and Colorado membership to perhaps 1,000. Locke, who by then had moved to 1605 Pennsylvania Street, continued to battle new and ultimately groundless tax evasion allegations. The IRS was embarrassed when its investigation not only failed to uncover any wrongdoing on the part of Locke, but discovered that he was actually owed a refund by the government for having paid too much in taxes. The *Denver Post* conceded that Locke's "personal integrity and underlying motives were above suspicion," and there was never any evidence that Locke had used the Klan or any other political movements for his own enrichment.

In 1934 he tried unsuccessfully to start a new and less divisive organization, the "Order of Equals," which included Catholics and Jews. But for Locke time was running out. On April Fool's day, 1935 he died of a heart attack at the Brown Palace Hotel while attending a political meeting.

He was buried at Fairmount Cemetery following a large funeral.

CHARLES C. GATES, SR.
1877–1961

For most of the twentieth century, one of Denver's largest and most successful businesses was the privately held Gates Rubber Company, whose sprawling factories dominated eighty acres and several city blocks near Interstate-25 and Broadway. At its peak, Gates was the city's largest employer and the country's sixth largest rubber manufacturer. Gates operated in several countries, employing more than 18,000 people worldwide, primarily producing rubber parts for the transportation industry: tires, belts, hoses, and transmission components.

The company was started in 1911 when the founder, Charles C. Gates, bought the Colorado Tire and Leather Company at Eleventh Avenue and Broadway for $3,500. In a day when automobiles were still in their infancy, some of the company's best-selling products were "Never-Break" elk leather horse halters, endorsed by Buffalo Bill Cody, and "Durable Tread" leather tire covers, which customers mounted over the unreliable rubber tires of the day to get extra mileage. As the automobile market grew, and the horse market dwindled, Gates shifted to making fan belts and rubber tires, eventually becoming the country's leading manufacturer of belts.

The company, renamed International Rubber Company, moved to its South Broadway location in 1914. Five years later the name was changed to Gates Rubber Company.

Charles Gates was born on November 26, 1877 in Waterford, Michigan, and received a mining degree from Michigan College of

169

Charles Gates posing with a few of his early
Gates Rubber products.
COURTESY OF THE COLORADO HISTORICAL SOCIETY, F39237.

Charles Gates's crypt at the Fairmount Mausoleum,
between those of his wife, Hazel, and his daughter, Ruth.

Mining and Technology in 1904. Like many Coloradans, Gates came west after graduation to work as a mining engineer. But after his 1910 marriage to a Denver native, twenty-year-old Hazel Rhoads, the thirty-two-year-old Gates began to tire of the amount of travel required of a mining and consulting engineer and decided to put his life savings into a local business that he and his wife, who was a bookkeeper, could run. A younger brother, John Gates, joined the company in 1912.

Gates's conservative, engineering-oriented management guided the company to year after year of steady profits, with no debt. Sales went from $264,000 in 1914 to over $6 million in 1931, and more than $100 million by the 1950s. Health problems in the 1940s forced him to begin spending winters at his home in Hawaii, but even there he continued to put in a full working day on company business, and he remained active and in charge until his death. In the days before faxes and the internet, business was conducted by phone and special delivery airmail between Hawaii and Denver.

In the summer of 1961 Gates was back in Denver. The company had marked its fiftieth birthday in March, although Gates's health had prevented him from attending the celebration. On August 29 he died of heart failure at the age of eighty-three at his home at 2750 East Seventh Avenue. Despite his age and illness, at the time of his death he was still president of the company. He is buried at the Fairmount Mausoleum along with his wife, who died in 1972.

Charles and Hazel Gates had seven children, and it was their oldest son, Charles C. Gates, Jr., who succeeded his father as head of the company in September 1961. Faced with an increasingly stagnant and over-crowded market for its rubber products, the younger Gates embarked on a program of both expansion and diversification. Among the companies acquired by Gates were Learjet Corporation, General Electric's rechargeable battery business, Uniroyal's transmission belt business, and a broad variety of other businesses ranging from egg farming to mutual funds. Not all succeeded, but on balance the diversification effort paid off, and as a result Gates Rubber was able to top $1 billion in sales by the late 1980s.

By the 1990s, however, Gates Rubber had closed most of its Denver manufacturing operations, which had been rendered uneconomical as a result of lower production costs in other parts of the world. In 2003, the company officially ended all operations at the South Broadway location and moved its offices to downtown Denver.

In 1996 Gates Rubber was sold to Tomkins PLC, a British firm, for $1.16 billion. Today, the company still makes industrial and automobile hoses and also supplies the automobile industry with interior panels and trunk liners and produces a line of original equipment and replacement products under the Trico name. Gates Rubber has more than ninety factories and distribution centers in eighteen countries and employs more than 23,000 people. Sales are estimated to be approximately $3 billion annually.

Gates had supported a variety of community organizations, including the University of Denver and the Museum of Nature and Science. The Gates fortune also made possible the Gates Family Foundation, created in 1946, and Colorado's seventh largest charitable organization.

$\mathcal{J}$ESSE SHWAYDER
1882–1970

One of Denver's best-known companies, and at one time the world's largest luggage firm, had its origins in 1910 when Jesse Shwayder decided to put most of his life's savings, approximately $1,000, into starting a company in Denver to manufacture luggage. Shwayder had been selling luggage since 1903, when he entered the retail luggage business in Denver. By 1910 he was one of the country's top luggage salesmen, running a store in New York, and making a good living selling trunks and suitcases made by Seward Trunk and Bag Company.

Neither Shwayder, nor his family, which helped fund his new company, had any experience in manufacturing, and Denver was considered a remote and unpromising location for such a business. But Shwayder, who in 1907 had married a Colorado native, Nellie Weitz, was tired of living in New York and tired of working for others. He was later quoted as saying "It couldn't be done. Except I didn't know that, so I did it." And so, on March 10, 1910, the doors opened on South Santa Fe Drive for Shwayder Trunk Manufacturing Company, later Shwayder Brothers, and still later, the Samsonite Corporation.

Jesse Shwayder was born on March 26, 1882, in Blackhawk, Colorado, the son of a Polish immigrant storekeeper. The Blackhawk–Central City area was still fairly prosperous, although productive gold mining was rapidly coming to an end. In 1888 Jesse's father, Isaac, decided to move to Denver and go into business

An early 1920s promotional photo designed to demonstrate
graphically the strength of the Shwayder luggage. The photo shows
Jesse Shwayder and his four brothers atop a Shwayder suitcase. The
brothers are, from left to right, Mark, Maurice, Ben, Jesse, and Sol.

for himself, first with a grocery store, then with a used furniture business at Eighteenth and Larimer Streets. Jesse helped the family finances by selling newspapers on the street and singing in the choir at St. John's Episcopal Cathedral, where he was paid fifty cents every Sunday. After his graduation from West High School he worked with his father in the furniture business before opening a small luggage store in 1903 at Fifteenth and Curtis Streets. Shwayder did so well in the retail luggage business that by 1910 he was able to begin manufacturing his own line of luggage, and hired his father and brother—beginning a tradition that would be followed in later years as many of Jesse Shwayder's relatives worked for the closely held company.

Shwayder Trunk proved successful, although it took three years to show its first profit. In the 1920s most quality luggage still was made out of leather or cloth, but Shwayder's flagship product, a line of low-cost, matching luggage, was made of inexpensive paper fiber. To help convince people of the durability of a product that originally sold for $4.95 and was essentially made of processed paper, Shwayder created advertising campaigns featuring photographs of himself and his four brothers—almost 1,000 pounds of Shwayders—standing balanced on a board atop a single suitcase. Later, and to reinforce the image of durability, the luggage acquired the brand name "Samsonite," named after Samson, one of Jesse Shwayder's favorite Biblical characters. Eventually, Samsonite luggage was made out of wood and, ultimately, metal and plastic, but Samsonite's advertising always stressed the durability of the products, no matter what their composition. The slogan "Strong enough to stand on," which began in the 1920s, continued to be a company trademark.

In the 1930s the company began making folding furniture, including a very popular line of steel card tables and folding chairs. At its peak, the Samsonite plant at Broadway and Mississippi Avenue in Denver, next to Gates Rubber Company, made more luggage than any other manufacturer—turning out almost 18,000 pieces a day. In the 1950s Samsonite introduced the first luggage without the traditional wooden box frame, an ultralight design using a magnesium frame with recessed handles and rounded corners. In the 1960s the company again introduced a number of innovative and successful products, including a durable and lightweight attaché case and a line of injection-molded polypropylene luggage. At this time the company changed its name from Shwayder Brothers to Samsonite. In the 1970s the company began selling soft-sided and folding luggage—an effort that culminated in 1984 when the company purchased Lark, a high-end manufacturer of soft-sided luggage.

Although Jesse Shwayder relinquished direct control over the company to his son King in 1960, he continued to be active in the business and worked out of his old office on Broadway until he was well into his eighties. He and his wife lived on a 215-acre estate at 7000 West Jewell Avenue. Although the estate was adjacent to Green Gables Country Club, where Shwayder belonged, it featured its own, private nine-hole golf course.

Shwayder's father Isaac had been educated as a rabbi, and Shwayder was one of the area's largest contributors to Jewish charities. The Jesse and Nellie Shwayder Foundation has continued these charitable activities.

Jesse Shwayder died on July 24, 1970, at the age of eighty-eight at his home. He is buried in the Emanuel section of Fairmount Cemetery.

In 1973, three years after Shwayder's death, his company was acquired by Beatrice Foods, which then sold Samsonite in 1987 as part of what was then the largest corporate leveraged buyout in history. Today, Samsonite is an independent, publicly held company, with more than 5,000 employees, annual sales of almost $750 million, and operations throughout the world. The company headquarters is still in Denver, although manufacturing is done elsewhere, and the Shwayder family is no longer involved in the business. The last family member to head the business was Irving "Bud" Shwayder, a nephew of Jesse Shwayder, who was president until the change of ownership in 1987.

The grave of Jesse Shwayder, in the Emanuel section of Fairmount Cemetery.

During World War II, **Governor Carr** posed for this publicity
photo, riding to work with a state trooper on a bicycle built
for two, in an effort to show support for gasoline rationing.
COURTESY OF THE COLORADO HISTORICAL SOCIETY, F39576.

*R*ALPH L. CARR
1887–1950

As governor of Colorado for two terms from 1939 to 1943, Ralph Carr provided a clear—and rare—example of courageous political leadership. Carr's strong stand on one particular issue of principle was so unpopular that it would put an end to his promising political career.

Carr was born on December 11, 1887, in Rosita, Colorado, and grew up near Cripple Creek, where his father worked in the mines. He received his undergraduate degree from the University of Colorado in 1910 and a law degree in 1912. In 1913 he married Gretchen Fowler of Colorado Springs.

For several years, Carr combined his law practice with journalism, as editor and publisher for newspapers in Trinidad, Victor, and Antonito. Gradually, journalism gave way to interests in water law and then politics—first as a county attorney in Conejos County, then as an assistant attorney general, and finally as a United States Attorney. With the Democrat landslide of 1932, Carr, a Republican, returned to private practice. However, he remained interested in politics, particularly in the implications of Franklin Roosevelt's New Deal, which Carr believed represented a threat to individual rights and a shift of power away from local government and toward federal control.

By 1937, Colorado Republicans had lost five consecutive gubernatorial races. The administration of Democrat Teller Ammons, which was confronted by budget and tax issues exacerbated by the effects of the Great Depression, appeared vulnerable. The Republicans decided to nominate Carr, a fiscal conservative, and in the 1938 election he defeated Ammons.

Carr's first term was successful, and not particularly controversial, and his policy of fiscal restraint brought the state's budget into balance. Although he was usually at odds with Washington on many issues, his pro-states' rights positions were not out of the ordinary for Coloradans of both parties, who had little use for the New Deal. Indeed, in the 1940 presidential election, Republican Wendell Wilkie was supported not only by Carr, but also by Colorado's leading Democrat, Senator Ed Johnson. Colorado was one of a handful of states that were carried by Wilkie against the Roosevelt landslide, and Carr easily won reelection as governor.

If it had not been for what happened on December 7, 1941, Carr's tenure as governor, and Carr himself, might have passed quietly into history. Such was not to be the case.

Following the attack on Pearl Harbor, a wave of anti-Japanese feeling swept the country. Most people were fearful of a Japanese invasion of the West Coast, aided by supposedly disloyal Japanese Americans or "Nisei," a term for second generation, American-born Japanese. Despite having been branded as "enemies," by mainstream publications such as the *Denver Post,* there was never credible evidence for the level of fear that developed about the loyalty of Japanese-Americans. Nevertheless, the hysteria gathered momentum—culminating in President Roosevelt's Executive Order 9066 for the wholesale removal and relocation of Japanese-Americans from the West Coast. Perhaps because he had gotten to know and respect Nisei in rural Colorado, or perhaps because he believed so strongly in the Constitution, Carr reacted differently. He took an early—and lonely—position criticizing the lack of due process in Roosevelt's order. Carr recognized the Nisei's loyalty to the United States, and offered to open Colorado to citizens of Japanese descent, at least as a temporary refuge and home during the war.

Carr's position was not only unpopular with most Coloradans, but with his other fellow governors who expressed concern about allowing Nisei to live freely within their states.

It became clear to the federal government that relocation would have to mean incarceration. Beginning in 1942, more than 120,000 Nisei were forcibly removed from their homes and relocated to isolated internment camps, including one in southeastern Colorado, often losing their property and their rights in the process.

Carr continued to speak out on the issue, warning of the dangers of a government-sponsored attack on the rights of any group. He even hired a Nisei internee to live at his home and work as a housekeeper while attending school. Although few other politicians sided with Carr, he was not totally alone. The state's major universities, as well as many religious organizations, advocated fair treatment for the Nisei.

The gravesite of Governor Ralph Carr and
his wife Gretchen Carr at Fairmount Cemetery.

In 1942, Carr learned the political cost of advocating such an unpopular cause. He challenged incumbent Ed Johnson in that year's senatorial election. Johnson, who had strongly supported the internment camps, defeated Carr by a slim margin despite the fact that the Republicans won virtually every other race.

Leaving politics behind, Carr moved to Rangely, near the Utah border, where he resumed his previous careers as a water lawyer and a newspaperman, buying a part-interest in the weekly *Rangely News.*

In 1950, Carr died. He is buried at Fairmount Cemetery with his wife, Gretchen, who died in 1937. His courageous opposition to the internment camps is remembered in a memorial at Sakura Square in Denver, a plaque at the state capitol, and in numerous other tributes which have—belatedly—been paid to him.

In the end, of course, Carr's position proved to be not only principled, but also correct. There was virtually no evidence, credible or otherwise, of disloyalty by the overwhelming majority of Nisei, 33,000 of whom served with distinction in the United States armed forces during the war. Forty-three years after the war, Carr's lonely and unpopular stand received official vindication. In the Civil Liberties Act of 1988, Congress provided compensation for those whose rights had been violated, declared that there had never been any justification for the internment, and recognized that in fact the internees had been "victims of discrimination by the Federal Government." Upon signing the act, President Ronald Reagan said, "Here we admit a wrong. Here we affirm our commitment as a nation to equal justice under the law."

$\mathcal{B}$URNHAM F. HOYT
1887–1960

Few architects have had as significant and lasting an impact on the regions where they practiced as Burnham Hoyt had on the front range of Colorado in the twentieth century. At least a dozen of Hoyt's designs have earned landmark or historic designations.

Hoyt was born in Denver in 1887 and graduated from North High School. When he was twenty-one his brother Merrill, who was six years older and a practicing Denver architect, recognized his younger brother's talents and recommended he go to New York City to study. Hoyt left his job as a draftsman at a Denver architectural firm and enrolled at the Beaux-Arts Institute of Design in New York. He had an opportunity to work with some of the city's best architects, including Bertram G. Goodhue, a nationally known architect whose works include the Nebraska State Capitol and St. Bartholomew's Episcopal Church at Fifty-First Street and Park Avenue in New York, both historic landmark buildings.

After serving in the army in World War I, Hoyt returned to Denver in 1919 and, at the age of thirty-two, joined his brother's firm as a partner. During the 1920s, the firm designed a number of significant Denver buildings, including private homes, the Fourth Church of Christ, Scientist, in west Denver, the Park Hill Public Library on Montview Boulevard, Lake Junior High School, and the Denver Press Club. In 1927 Hoyt received a commission from John D. Rockefeller to design the Riverside Church in Morningside

Architect **Burnham Hoyt.**
COURTESY OF COLORADO HISTORICAL SOCIETY, F35433.

Burnham Hoyt's ashes were scattered in this northwestern
area of Fairmount Cemetery.

Heights in New York City, and soon after that left Denver to accept an appointment to the faculty of the New York University School of Architecture and to work on the Rockefeller project.

Hoyt's career as a New York-based architect was cut short in 1933 by the death of his brother, who died of a heart attack at the age of fifty-two. Hoyt felt an obligation to return to Denver to complete the work that was in progress at the firm when his brother died. In 1936, at the age of forty-nine, he married Mildred Fuller, and the decision was made to stay in Denver and concentrate his practice in the area.

Hoyt's architectural practice was highly successful. The core of his work was designing homes for Denver's wealthy, including the Waring House on Hawthorn Place, the Gano House at 101 High Street, the Maer House at 545 Circle Drive, and his own house at 3130 East Exposition.

However, he also did notable public and commercial work, including significant additions to the Central City Opera House and the Broadmoor Hotel, and his last commission—the original Denver Public Library at Fourteenth and Broadway. But certainly his most famous work was Red Rocks Amphitheater in Morrison. Built at the close of the Great Depression, the dream was that of George Cranmer, Denver's manager of parks, but the design was Hoyt's, and the labor was that of the Civilian Conservation Corps, a Great Depression–era federal agency that put unemployed people to work on public projects. Hoyt's dramatic design took advantage of the natural setting and materials and was a popular and critical success, receiving national recognition from New York's Museum of Modern Art and inclusion in the National Register of Historic Places.

By the time Hoyt had completed his work for the Denver Public Library's central building in the early 1950s, he had been diagnosed with Parkinson's disease, and by 1955, when the building opened, the illness forced him to retire. He lived for five more years, before dying at his Denver home in 1960 at the age of seventy-three. Hoyt's 1955 Denver Library building now is the northeast component of the new Central Library, designed by Michael Graves and the Denver firm of Klipp Colussy Jenks DuBois.

Somewhat curiously for an architect—and unlike fellow architect Frank Edbrooke who designed his own private mausoleum—Hoyt did not want a physical gravesite memorial of any kind. His ashes were scattered in an area in the northwest part of Fairmount Cemetery.

OLIVER E. "THE GHOST" MARCELLE
1897–1949

Oliver Marcelle starred as a third-baseman in the Negro Baseball Leagues in the 1920s and retired to Denver in 1933, where he was instrumental in bringing Black professional baseball to the city.

Marcelle was born in Thibodaux, Louisiana, in 1897 and began his professional career with the Brooklyn Royal Giants in 1918, when he was twenty-one. In the 1920s he starred with the Atlantic City Bacharach Giants, the New York Lincoln Giants, and the Baltimore Black Sox. He was captain for Atlantic City in the 1926 Black World Series. At Baltimore, Marcelle was part of the so-called "Million Dollar Infield" with Dick Lundy, Jud Wilson, and Frank Warfield. The term "Million Dollar Infield" referred not to what they were paid, which was very little, but to what observers felt the infield would be worth in the major leagues—if they were white ballplayers.

Although Marcelle was a strong hitter, batting .362 in 1922 and having a career average of .305, he was considered to be even better defensively. He is frequently listed as one of the top third-basemen ever to play in the Negro Leagues, comparing favorably with Ray Dandridge and Judy Johnson, both members of the Baseball Hall of Fame. The origin of his nickname, "The Ghost," is uncertain, but some say it may have resulted from the way he seemed to be everywhere on the left side of the infield. Marcelle played third base much nearer to home plate than most other players and that, coupled with

Oliver Marcelle.
COURTESY OF THE NEGRO LEAGUE BASEBALL PLAYERS ASSOCIATION.

Oliver E. "The Ghost" Marcelle's
gravesite in Riverside Cemetery.

his quickness, enabled him to stop most balls hit to the left side.

Marcelle had a quick temper, which sometimes resulted in fights. One such fight, in 1930, led to Marcelle's leaving baseball prematurely. He and his teammate Frank Warfield were shooting dice one day in Cuba during winter league play when they got into an argument that ended with Warfield biting off part of Marcelle's nose.

Marcelle tried to continue his career, wearing a black nose patch, but he was a vain man—indeed had been considered a handsome man—and wasn't able to withstand the kidding he received as a result of his injury. Even after his retirement he usually wore a patch and was known in his Denver neighborhood not as "The Ghost," but "The Patch."

The Denver to which Marcelle moved in the 1930s was, like the rest of the country, a place where segregation dictated that black and white players could not play on the same team and, frequently, could not even play against one another. Denver was remote and far removed from the famous teams and big names of baseball. Colorado sports fans had to be satisfied with the minor leagues, and only occasional visits by barnstorming stars such as Babe Ruth and Lou Gehrig playing exhibition games with hastily thrown together "teams" such as the Denver Buicks, the Denver Skyscrapers, or the Milliken Whizbangs. The biggest baseball event in the area was the semi-pro *Denver Post* Tournament, which was held at Merchants Park at Broadway and Exposition Avenue. It was this event that attracted Marcelle's attention, and he convinced Poss Parsons, a sports writer for the *Denver Post* to invite the Black Kansas City Monarchs, and future Hall-of-Famer Satchel Paige, to play in the tournament. As a result, Black baseball came to Denver's most prestigious baseball event, and the following year, the tournament began to include integrated teams.

But, after the 1934 *Denver Post* Tournament, Marcelle faded from the sports scene. He became a day laborer and a house painter, and a lifetime of heavy drinking began to take its toll. Out of money, out of touch with his family, and suffering from acute heart disease, he died in 1949 at the age of fifty-two and was buried in an unmarked "pauper's grave" on the west side of Riverside Cemetery.

Many years later, Jay Sanford, who had lived in New Orleans, near where Marcelle was from, and was a Denver area businessman and sports historian, heard about Marcelle's fate. He spearheaded an effort to gain belated recognition for Marcelle, and solicited the cooperation of the departing minor league Denver Zephyrs and the incoming major league Colorado Rockies.

As a result of these efforts, on June 1, 1991, ninety-four years after Marcelle's birth and forty-two years after his burial, a ceremony at Riverside Cemetery unveiled his new tombstone. "I was glad to see they did this for Ollie, he was out there in an unmarked grave," said Buck O'Neil, one of the legends of the Negro Leagues and the chairman of the board of the Negro Leagues Museum in Kansas City. O'Neil, who knew Marcelle when both were with the Miami Giants at the twilight of Marcelle's career and the beginning of O'Neil's, contributed this quotation to the tombstone: "Baseball's best third baseman brought professional baseball to Colorado." Marcelle was named to the Louisiana Sports Hall of Fame in 1996.

Maurice B. Rose
1899–1945

As the United States Army pushed into
Germany in the last days of World War II, among the casualties was
Major General Maurice Rose, one of the army's most decorated soldiers. He was one of the highest-ranking officers—and the only
armored division commander—to be killed in the war. In the words
of *Chicago Sun* war correspondent Thomas Henry, Rose's death was
the "greatest single loss" suffered by the Army. Rose Medical Center
in Denver was named in his honor.

Rose was born in Connecticut on November 26, 1899, the
grandson of an Orthodox rabbi who had immigrated from Poland.
The family moved to Denver when Maurice was three. His father
went into the clothing business, and Maurice lived in east-central
Denver and graduated from East High School.

As a child he showed a strong interest in military history, and
when he was fifteen he joined the National Guard, hoping to take
part in General Pershing's foray into Mexico, in retaliation for a raid
by Pancho Villa. Rose was sent home when it was discovered he was
underage. However, in 1917 he was accepted in officer school and
was commissioned as a lieutenant in the infantry. In 1918 he went to
France, where he was wounded in combat during World War I.

After the war ended, Rose left the army and returned to Denver,
where he worked as a salesman. He found civilian life unsatisfying,
and in 1920 he rejoined the army. During the twenty-year interlude
between the World Wars, Rose served in a variety of locations,

Taken just seventeen days before his death, this photo shows **General Rose** in a characteristic scene: wearing combat gear and using the walkie-talkie from his jeep near the front of the battle.
COURTESY OF THE COLORADO HISTORICAL SOCIETY, 86.296.37.

General Rose's grave is marked with flowers in this 1960 Veteran's Day tribute at the cemetery in Margraten, Holland.
COURTESY OF THE COLORADO HISTORICAL SOCIETY.

including at the Command and General Staff School and at Fort Logan in Colorado. He transferred from infantry to cavalry and, eventually, to tanks, and became skilled in the kind of armored warfare that would figure prominently in World War II. Although not as well known an armored commander as Rommel or Patton, Rose is considered by many historians to have been every bit their equal; he was certainly easier to get along with than Patton and, ultimately, more successful than Rommel.

It was in the few short years of America's involvement in World War II that Rose's place in history would be forged. He began as General Patton's Chief of Staff in 1942. In 1943 Rose received his first battlefield commands, first as a lieutenant colonel, then as a brigadier general, Rose was with the 1st and 2nd Armored Divisions as they helped recapture North Africa from the Germans, and he achieved the war's first unconditional surrender of a German division.

Following the African campaign, Rose led the successful attack on Sicily's capital, Palermo, in the summer of 1943. In Rose's case the term "led the attack," is not a figure of speech. Unlike generals who directed their division's engagements from well behind the lines, Rose preferred to be at the front with his troops—usually in a jeep. By late 1943 he was in England preparing for D-Day, and he had received two Silver Stars for gallantry in action.

On June 7, 1944, Rose led the advance unit of the 2nd Armored Division into France, engaging German troops in costly "hedgerow" fighting in Normandy and playing a key role in preventing a successful counterattack. In August, Rose was promoted to major general—the third highest rank in the Army—and given command of the 3rd Armored "Spearhead" Division, a unit that was considered to be the most powerful armored force in the world. For the next eight months, the 3rd was continuously engaged in combat, driving the Germans out of France, Belgium, and Holland, and becoming the first American armored division to enter Germany and the first Allied unit to capture a German city. For these campaigns, Rose received the Distinguished Service Cross, the nation's second highest military honor. In December 1944 and January 1945, the 3rd Division swung around from inside the German border to help turn back the desperate counterattack that became known as the Battle of the Bulge, the largest land battle of the war involving American troops.

With the defeat of the German counter-offensive in the west, and the approach of the Russians from the east, it became clear that Germany's days were numbered. The 3rd Armored quickly moved deep into Germany. On the night of March 30 the division was facing a large German armored unit. General Rose, characteristically at the head of the attacking force, encountered a German tank. One vehicle in Rose's contingent got away, but his jeep was trapped. In the dark, and the heat of battle, no one knows the details of what happened next. Was Rose trying to release his gun belt and surrender? Did the young German tank commander believe Rose was reaching for his gun? Whatever the case, the German tank commander, who has never been identified, fired his automatic weapon, and Rose was killed instantly. Twelve days later, the 3rd Armored would liberate the notorious Dora-Mittelbau, a sub-camp of the Buchenwald concentration camp, where the Germans had been using slave labor to build V-2 rockets. Twenty-three days later the 3rd Armored was withdrawn from battle, and thirty-eight days later Germany surrendered.

General Rose was buried in Germany then relocated to the American Military Cemetery at Margraten, Netherlands, alongside many of the 3,000 other soldiers of the 3rd Armored who died in battle. Denver's Jewish community named the hospital they built in 1948 in his honor. In a curious footnote, however, there was confusion about Rose's religious affiliation at the time of death—and when this uncertainty came to the attention of the Jewish community members that were raising money for the hospital, there was some controversy.

Rose's gravesite was first marked by a cross, then a Star of David, and finally, again, a cross, which remains to this day and reflects the fact that an official Army inquiry determined that he had in fact changed religions. According to authors Steven Ossad and Don Marsh, in their biography of Rose, he made the change early in his army career, perhaps as early as 1918, when he was nineteen years old.

The reasons for the change are obscure and, as far as can be determined, were never explained by Rose or communicated to his deeply religious parents. As an adult, however, he apparently paid little attention to organized religion of any kind, although when he did so he attended Protestant services, and his second wife, Virginia, was a Catholic. It has also been speculated that he may have felt that his chances for advancement in the army would be improved by such a change of religion, although there were many Jewish senior officers, including generals and admirals, who served before and during the time Rose was in the army.

In any event, the Denver Jewish community decided to proceed as originally planned, choosing to honor Rose's Jewish heritage and ignore any controversy over his subsequent religious life. On August 31, 1948, General Rose Memorial Hospital was dedicated by Rose's commander, General Dwight D. Eisenhower.

Although there remains confusion about the events surrounding Rose's death, and about his attitude toward religion, there is no uncertainty about his bravery, leadership, and contribution to the Nazi defeat. He was a genuine hero and was loved and admired by his men, who paid him their highest compliment: General Rose was "a soldier's soldier."

Dr. Florence Sabin in the lab.
COURTESY OF THE COLORADO HISTORICAL SOCIETY, F23991, F2241.

Florence Sabin is entombed alongside her
sister Mary Sophia at Fairmount Mausoleum.

$\mathcal{F}$LORENCE RENA SABIN
1871–1953

Two Coloradans are memorialized in the National Statuary Hall collection in the Capitol in Washington: former astronaut Jack Swigert, and medical research pioneer Florence Rena Sabin. It was Sabin's post-retirement career in public health that reformed Colorado's notoriously poor health-care system in the 1940s.

Sabin was a Colorado native. Her father, an engineer who had originally planned to be a doctor, came west from Vermont looking for gold in 1860. He eventually settled in Central City, where he met and married Serena Miner, who had come west from Georgia to teach school in Blackhawk. Florence was born on November 9, 1871. Her mother died when she was eight, and her father faced the difficult decision of finding the best way to raise his daughters. Initially, Florence and her sister, Mary, were sent to an Episcopal boarding school, Wolfe Hall, located in what is now downtown Denver. From Denver they were moved on to Chicago, where they lived with their uncle and his family, and finally to the Sabin family farm in Saxton's River, Vermont, where they lived with their paternal grandparents. It was there that Florence began to learn more about her ancestors, including several who had been doctors. They were all, of course, men. At that time women doctors were rare—indeed, it was not until 1849 that a woman graduated from medical school in the United States—and Sabin's grandmother remarked sadly to her one day that it was a shame Florence was a woman because she would have made make a good doctor.

Despite the frequent moves, the Sabin girls received good basic educations and were admitted to Smith College in Northampton, Massachusetts, where Florence and her sister excelled. After college, Sabin returned to Colorado, where her father still lived. She taught for a few years at Wolfe Hall and then at Smith College, saving her money for what had become the overriding goal of her life: to become a doctor. In 1896 she took the first step when she entered Johns Hopkins Medical School. Although at that time women were, for the most part, still not allowed to attend medical schools, Johns Hopkins had recently received a gift that required it to admit women. This enabled Florence to become one of the first women to enter the school and in 1900 she graduated at the top of her class.

Following medical school, Sabin began a distinguished academic career at Johns Hopkins: she not only taught but also conducted medical research, including research centered on the embryological origins of the lymphatic system. She later worked on the origins of blood, blood cells, and blood vessels, on the histology of the brain, and on the pathology and immunology of tuberculosis. She was the first woman to become a professor at the school and was a prominent supporter of women's rights. In 1924 she moved to New York's Rockefeller Institute for Medical Research to direct the Department of Cellular Studies. She was the first woman to be a department head at the Institute, and conducted significant research in several areas, including the lymphatic system, blood vessels and cells, and tuberculosis. According to Jeanne Varnell, who wrote about Sabin in her 1999 book *Women of Consequence,* the head of the Rockefeller Institute had called Sabin "the leading woman scientist in the world."

Sabin retired, for the first time, in 1938 and moved back to Colorado. She was sixty-seven. Her career thus far, though clearly notable, did not yet relate to Colorado. She lived for several years with her sister at 1333 East Tenth Avenue in Denver's Cheesman Park neighborhood but frequently returned to the east for advanced research activities at the Rockefeller Institute.

It was following World War II that Florence Sabin embarked on an unlikely and equally significant second career: reforming Colorado's public health system.

She got involved as a result of an ironic political situation. In 1944 Colorado Governor John Vivian appointed a blue-ribbon postwar committee to help the state plan for the transition from war to peace. No sooner had the committee been named than a reporter pointed out to the governor that the committee appeared to have two weaknesses: there was no member for health care and there was no woman. Anxious to avoid the potential controversy, Vivian decided to kill two birds with one stone, and appointed the seventy-three-year-old Sabin to head the health-care taskforce. If being a woman had been an obstacle early in her career, in 1944 it proved to be an asset. Knowing little about Sabin other than her gender and her age, Vivian mistakenly expected her simply to be a figurehead.

He was wrong. Working first with Vivian, and then with a series of more responsive elected officials, including Vivian's successor, Governor Lee Knous, and Denver Mayor Quigg Newton, Sabin determined to improve the state's health policies and practices, which were among the worst in the nation at the time.

Health-care reform legislation was introduced in General Assembly, and Sabin campaigned successfully throughout the state for the passage of the laws, which created modern standards and independent and effective health departments. She then headed both the state Board of Health and, later, the Denver Department of Health and Charities where Sabin eliminated a long-standing political patronage system under which Denver General Hospital and the city's overall health-care systems had suffered. Sabin introduced improvements in virtually every area of health care, including sanitation standards, enforcement of communicable disease laws, and the creation of more comprehensive health programs for children.

She officially retired in 1951 at the age of 80 and died two years later, on October 3, 1953, while listening to the radio broadcast of game four of the Yankees–Dodgers World Series. While living in New York, Sabin had become an avid Brooklyn Dodgers fan, and it is likely that her last thoughts were pleasant ones. The pitching of Billy Loes, as well as a Duke Snider home run, helped lead the Dodgers to a 7–3 victory over the Yankees to tie the series at two games apiece. It would be the highpoint for the Dodgers, who lost the next two games and the Series.

Florence Sabin accumulated an impressive array of accomplishments and honors in addition to her statue in the nation's capital. She was the recipient of honorary degrees from fifteen universities and was the first female lifetime member of the National Academy of Science. Denver's Sabin Elementary School was named after her, as was the Sabin Cancer Research Wing at the University of Colorado's Denver Medical Center. She is also the only Colorado woman to be included in the American Women of Achievement book series, joining forty-nine other notable women, including Helen Keller, Margaret Mead, and Eleanor Roosevelt.

Her ashes are entombed at Fairmount Mausoleum.

*J*AMES JOHNSTON WARING
1883–1962

Dr. James J. Waring, the first full-time professor of medicine at the University of Colorado Health Sciences Center, left an impressive and continuing legacy within the state's medical community, including the Webb-Waring Institute.

Waring was born on August 11, 1883, in Savannah, Georgia. His parents were Anne Waring, the eldest daughter of a prominent Savannah doctor, and Antonio de Gorgoza, who was born in Spain and immigrated to the United States in the 1870s. Despite strong opposition from Anne's father, Waring's parents were married in 1881 and had two boys, James and Antonio. The marriage must have been a tumultuous one. Gorgoza was a heavy drinker who conducted several extra-marital affairs and refused to speak to his father-in-law—except to threaten to shoot him. Anne's father was an outspoken man, unlikely to be able to keep his opinions of Anne's husband to himself. The marriage ended in divorce in 1889. Anne reclaimed her maiden name, and her son James J. de Gorgoza became James J. Waring.

James Waring was educated in Savannah and at Lawrenceville boarding school in New Jersey before entering Yale, from which he was graduated in 1904. Like his maternal grandfather and great-grandfather he decided to study medicine and enrolled at Johns Hopkins. It was there, in Baltimore, that he contracted tuberculosis, the leading cause of death in the United States at that time. Treatment in those days was uncertain and often involved moving to different climates. Colorado was one of the most popular destina-

Dr. James Waring and his wife, Ruth Waring.
Rocky Mountain News photo.
COURTESY OF THE DENVER PUBLIC LIBRARY, WESTERN
HISTORY COLLECTION, RMN 978.

James Waring is buried at the Waring and
White family gravesite at Fairmount Cemetery.

tions for tuberculosis patients, and in 1908 Waring entered a treatment center, or sanatorium, in Colorado Springs. One of the twenty-five-year-old Waring's doctors was Englishman Gerald B. Webb.

By 1911 Waring had recovered sufficiently to return to medical school at the University of Colorado, from which he graduated in 1913. In 1914 he began teaching part-time at the school, while also beginning his private practice—specializing in treatment of the many tuberculosis patients who had come to Colorado. He also began collecting medical history books and writing scholarly papers, frequently about tuberculosis and other diseases of the chest.

In 1920 Waring met Ruth Porter, daughter of Henry M. Porter, a prominent businessman who had made a fortune in ranching and real estate. They were married in 1921. Their house, at 910 Gaylord Street, was designed for them by Jacques Benedict and has been designated a landmark by the Denver Landmark Preservation Commission. The couple had two daughters, Ruth and Anne. In 1926 Waring became an assistant professor at the University of Colorado medical school, which had just opened its new facilities at Ninth Avenue and Colorado Boulevard in Denver. During the 1920s Waring, who was president of the Denver Public Health Council and Denver Medical Society, lobbied for better treatment facilities for tuberculosis patients. He had hoped that his father-in-law would donate funds toward such a facility. However, in 1928 Henry Porter decided to start a general hospital instead, and in 1930 the doors of Porter Hospital were opened. Waring, who in 1935 was elected president of the National Tuberculosis Association, never succeeded in getting the kind of public sanatorium he wanted in Colorado, defeated by a combination of lack of interest on the part of policy makers and the reduced need for such facilities because of improvements in the prevention and treatment of the disease.

In 1933 Waring became head of the department of medicine at the University of Colorado, a position he would hold until 1948. He was also its first "full-time" professor. Waring, however, continued to maintain a private internal medicine practice, necessitated by the fact that until 1941 the teaching positions he held—like many such positions in medical schools at that time—were unpaid.

Waring had occasion frequently to work with Gerald Webb, the Colorado Springs doctor who had treated him when he first came to Colorado. After Webb's death in 1948, Waring took over Webb's position as head of the Colorado Foundation for Research in Tuberculosis (CFRT), and was deeply involved in the development of new drug treatments for the disease. After relinquishing his administrative duties in 1948, Waring continued to teach at the medical school until 1952. Hands-on classroom teaching and clinical diagnostics were his first loves.

In 1953 he was awarded the Trudeau Medal, the highest award offered by the American Thoracic Society, a branch of the American Lung Association, and in 1955 former students and associates created the Waring Society at the medical school, an honorary society for medical students. Also in 1953 construction began at the medical school on a new building for the CFRT, which opened in 1954. In 1959 the name of the CFRT was changed to the Webb Institute for Medical Research.

Waring, who had a history of heart problems as well as tuberculosis, died at his home in 1962 at the age of seventy-eight. Following his death, the Webb Institute was renamed in his honor, and is today the Webb-Waring Institute for Cancer, Aging, and Antioxidant Research. Waring's role in the development of the medical school also includes the Waring Collection of books about the history of medicine, which is housed at the university library, and the James J. Waring Endowed Chair for Experimental Medicine. He is buried at Fairmount Cemetery.

Ruth Waring, lived thirty-one more years and was active in a number of charities and civic organizations, including serving on the boards of the Denver Symphony and the Denver Botanic Gardens, of which she was a founder. She died at the age of 103 and is buried alongside her husband at Fairmount Cemetery.

$\mathcal{T}$EMPLE HOYNE BUELL
1895–1990

It was the prospect of improved health that brought Temple Buell to Denver from Chicago, where he had been born in 1895. Like many others with his respiratory condition—brought on as a result of having been subjected to a poison gas attack in France during World War I—he was told by doctors that he would benefit from the Colorado climate. Buell came to Colorado in 1921—the same year he married Marjorie McIntosh, an heir to the Household Finance fortune, and the first of Buell's three wives. By the time of his death in 1990, he had helped change the face of Denver forever.

"Sandy" Buell, as he was called because of his prominent red moustache, created one of the region's largest architectural firms and was involved with several projects that remain historically significant landmarks today. Among these are the Paramount Theater, the Colorado State Services Building at Colfax Avenue and Sherman Street, and many schools, including Horace Mann Junior High School.

Ultimately, however, Buell's greatest impact on Denver came from real estate projects not architectural ones. Buell was inspired by Kansas City developer J. C. Nichols, who in 1922 introduced the suburban shopping center concept. His Country Club Plaza proved that it was more than just another shopping center—it became the focal point for a major commercial area that rivaled, and in many ways eventually surpassed, the importance of the original core of downtown Kansas City.

Temple Buell as a young man in the 1920s.
COURTESY OF THE COLORADO HISTORICAL SOCIETY, F35430.

Nichols had started in 1905 by buying ten acres in what was then "rural" Kansas City. In 1925 Buell made the same kind of decision, buying forty-nine acres for $25,000 at the intersection of First Avenue and University Boulevard in Denver. Since there was no immediate demand for the land, Denver leased the property from Buell—for use as a town dump.

The area Buell had bought was as much rural as suburban. On the west side was the Denver Country Club, on the east the Polo Club—that at that time actually was a polo field, not a real estate development—and to the south ran Cherry Creek, as yet untamed by a dam. The rest of the area, which had been known as the town of Harmon until it was annexed by Denver in 1894, included a town hall at Fourth Avenue and St. Paul Street and a two-story schoolhouse where Bromwell Elementary School now stands. The area consisted primarily of truck farms and greenhouses.

By 1946, twenty years after Buell's purchase, Denver was beginning to grow around Buell's property. Aware of the success Nichols' Plaza was having in Kansas City, Buell decided to have the property developed as a shopping center. After enduring some lengthy zoning battles, construction began in 1949 and an anchor tenant, the Denver Dry Goods Company, opened in 1953 in a building that later became Bed, Bath & Beyond. Sears followed suit across First Avenue and the development of the Cherry Creek Shopping Center area was underway. Denver's southeastward move was solidified. In the late 1960s Buell tried, unsuccessfully, to add a seventeen-story medical center, a fifty-four-story office tower topped with a revolving restaurant, and underground parking for 16,000 cars. The plans were rejected by Denver planning and zoning departments.

Buell also was instrumental in the development of the Midtown Shopping Center in Pueblo, the Cherry Hills Country Club, and the Cherry Hills residential subdivision, where he bought 192 acres in the mid-1930s. He lived at the 14,400-square-foot "Buell Mansion" in Cherry Hills for much of his life, but he also had a large house adjacent to the Cherry Creek shopping center, at 106 South University Boulevard.

Later in life, Buell sought to add to his legacy through philanthropy. Not all of his efforts were successful. Colorado Women's College, which had been conceived as a "Vassar of the West" by its founder, opened in 1909 in northeast Denver. In 1967 the school changed its name to Temple Buell College, after Buell and his second wife announced plans for a $25 million gift. Buell had married Virginia Bennett, who worked as a volunteer at the college, in 1963, five years after a highly publicized divorce from his first wife. Under terms of the agreement with the college, Buell would arrange permanent funding for the institution and he and his wife would be buried in a monument on the campus. However, before the gift could be completed, the whole plan, as well as the Buell marriage, fell apart. First, the school's problems began to overwhelm it as debts increased and enrollment fell. Then, in 1971, Virginia and Temple Buell were divorced. In 1973, the school was renamed Colorado Women's College, and in 1982, it merged with the University of Denver. It is now a campus for Johnson and Wales University, offering courses specializing in business and culinary arts.

More successful was his work on behalf of the arts, as the benefactor of the Buell Theater at the Denver Center for the Performing Arts, and for his college and graduate schools, the University of Illinois and Columbia University. He donated funds for the construction of Buell Gallery in the University of Illinois architectural center and provided for the creation of a new architecture building, Buell Hall. At Columbia, he founded the Buell Center for the Study of American Architecture, part of the graduate school of architecture. In 1962 he founded the Temple Buell Foundation that, with more than $100 million in assets, specializes in early childhood education and development projects for children.

In 1975 Buell, then eighty, married Donna Sherry. Their marriage ended in another highly publicized divorce in 1985. Buell died in 1990 at the age of ninety-four at his Cherry Hills Village mansion and is buried at Fairmount Cemetery in one of the cemetery's largest and most elaborate private buildings.

The Buell Mausoleum at Fairmount Cemetery.

"Daddy" Bruce Randolph in 1984 at the dedication
of his street in northeast Denver.

"Daddy" Bruce Randolph's grave at Fairmount Cemetery.

"DADDY" BRUCE RANDOLPH
1900–1994

As the years pass by it is likely that most motorists driving in northeast Denver will have no difficulty recognizing the meaning and origins of Martin Luther King Boulevard. Such may not be the case with a street two blocks north named Bruce Randolph Avenue, which received its name in 1985, five years after East Thirty-Second Avenue was named for King.

Randolph didn't move to Denver until he was past sixty years of age. He was born in the tiny town of Pastoria, Arkansas, near Pine Bluff, on February 15, 1900. He left home at the age of fifteen for Little Rock, where he worked in mines as a water boy and mule driver. By the time he was twenty he had returned to Pastoria and was married in 1924. At that time prohibition was the law of the land, and Randolph supplemented his job as a barbecue chef by selling bootleg whiskey.

In 1933, following the death of his wife, Polly, he moved from Arkansas and settled in Pampa, a city in the Texas Panhandle not far from Amarillo, where he was remarried and owned several small businesses, including a barbecue restaurant. In 1958 he was divorced from his second wife and moved to Tucson, Arizona, where he again ran a barbecue restaurant, but it was not successful.

By 1960 the Tucson restaurant had closed, and Randolph moved one last time—to Denver, where his son had opened a barbershop.

When he arrived in Denver, Randolph was in his sixties and broke. He began working as a janitor and shining shoes to make ends meet. He also began doing again what he knew and liked best. He started a small, informal barbecue business based in his son's back yard, where he did some catering and cooking for friends and neighbors. In 1963 he made it official, opening Daddy Bruce's Bar-BQ at 1629 Thirty-Fourth Avenue, not far from his son's shop. In those days Southern-style barbecue was still fairly new to Denver, and Randolph's place did well, quickly becoming something of an institution in northeast Denver.

The financial side of running a restaurant was never as important to him as the food and the people—which was best illustrated by his reputation for never turning away a needy person who was hungry. This charitable impulse, founded in his religion, took root in Denver as he not only responded to requests for assistance but also organized and funded holiday meals for the hungry and the homeless—feeding hundreds of families with meals of turkey, ribs, yams, corn, beans, and pies. He didn't stop there. Before long he was organizing clothing drives and Easter egg hunts. Randolph's activities on behalf of the needy would continue for more than thirty years, even in times when he was experiencing severe financial difficulties. Gradually his reputation as "Daddy" Bruce the restaurateur was overshadowed by his reputation for selfless charity.

The downside of Randolph's charitable activities, combined with his casual approach to running a business, meant that despite the popularity of Daddy Bruce's Bar-BQ it never became a thriving business economically. Several times in the 1980s Daddy Bruce's was on the brink of bankruptcy. However, fittingly, on those occasions the community to which Randolph had given so much stepped in and raised money to satisfy creditors or tax collectors.

The doors stayed open until 1993 when failing health, advanced age, and continuing financial problems combined to force Randolph to close the east Denver restaurant and end his active participation in the annual holiday food events. Randolph died at a niece's home in Denver on March 18, 1994, just a month past his ninety-fourth birthday. His death resulted in a large and spontaneous outpouring of expressions of respect from a wide range of people, rich and poor, powerful and powerless.

The community mobilized to keep his memory and his charitable activities alive through the Daddy Bruce Foundation, headed by the Reverend Gill Ford. Organizations such as Conoco Phillips, Qwest, The Black McDonald's Operators Association, and KBCO-FM have joined with the Denver Broncos and other civic and business organizations, and hundreds of volunteers to maintain the holiday meal tradition that Bruce Randolph started. The program grew from providing food to about 900 families in its first year to more than 6,000, although as it grew larger the practice of serving hot dinners was replaced by distributing food baskets and, most recently, by giving out gift cards for food.

In addition to the dedication of Bruce Randolph Avenue, "Daddy" Bruce is remembered in the naming of the Bruce Randolph Middle School at 3100 East Fortieth Avenue, and Daddy Bruce–style barbecue lives on at his son's restaurant in Boulder.

He is buried at Fairmount Cemetery. According to his obituary in the *Rocky Mountain News,* he had written what he wanted to appear on his grave:

> *Bruce Randolph Sr.*
> *Feb. 15, 1900 – (?)* [sic]
> *God Loves You*
> *So Does Daddy Bruce*
> *It Is More Blessed To Give*
> *Than It Is To Receive.*

However, Daddy Bruce suffered the fate of most authors. Editing resulted in a slightly shorter epitaph, with one side of his tombstone bearing the words, "God loves you and so do I," and the other, shown here, "It is more blessed to give than receive."

Joe Holland.
COURTESY OF HOLLAND AND HART CLIENT SERVICES.

Stephen Hart.
COURTESY OF HOLLAND AND HART CLIENT SERVICES

$\mathcal{J}$OSIAH GILBERT HOLLAND
1900–1975

$\mathcal{S}$TEPHEN HARDING HART
1908–1993

For more than half a century the names Holland and Hart have stood out in legal circles in the Rocky Mountains as the area's largest firm, with more than 260 lawyers in 12 offices in Colorado, Wyoming, Idaho, Montana, New Mexico, Utah, and the District of Columbia.

The firm was born in 1947 when Stephen H. Hart and Josiah (Joe) G. Holland decided to leave their existing practices to create the new firm that would bear their names—with "Holland" coming first, in deference to him being the older of the two lawyers.

Both Steve Hart and Joe Holland were Denver natives, and their lives and careers followed remarkably similar paths. Holland was born in Denver on November 16, 1900, and was named after his grandfather, a well-known nineteenth century journalist, poet, and author who was one of the first biographers of Abraham Lincoln. His father, Theodore, was a lawyer, and Joe Holland followed in his footsteps, receiving his law degree from the University of Denver after doing his undergraduate work at the University of Colorado and Yale University. Holland began practicing law in 1925, and over the next twenty-two years he was associated with several firms, including Grant, Ellis, Shafroth, and Toll; Lewis, Bond, and Holland; and White and Holland.

Early in his career, he served for two years in the state legislature as a Republican representative from Denver and also worked as a mining manager during the Depression to help supplement the income from his law practice. The experience proved useful because mining and antitrust law were his specialties as a corporate trial lawyer.

Hart was born on April 13, 1908, and after attending Denver Public Schools he studied at Yale University, Oxford, and Harvard Law School, before returning to Denver to get his law degree at the University of Denver in 1933. The depths of the Depression were not an auspicious time to begin a private law practice, however, and Hart worked instead as a lawyer for the Department of the Interior before joining the law firm of Lewis and Grant, where he specialized in tax law. Hart's failure to be made a partner at Lewis and Grant was a major factor in his decision to strike out with Joe Holland and create the new firm that, to Hart's satisfaction, soon eclipsed his former employer in both size and influence.

Like Holland, Hart served briefly in the state legislature, although as a Democrat.

In addition to law, politics, Yale, and the University of Denver, Holland and Hart shared a love of the outdoors and were members of the Colorado Mountain Club. Before they made the decision to create their firm, they had become personal friends and frequently went on skiing, climbing, and whitewater rafting excursions in the mountains. They also shared an interest in the culture of the West. Holland collected Western art, and Hart served for fifty-five years on the board of the Colorado Historical Society, where two of his favorite projects were the successful restoration of the "Georgetown Loop" narrow-gauge railway from Georgetown to Silver Plume and the preservation of the Daniels and Fisher Tower from the plans of Denver Urban Renewal. The Colorado Historical Society's library is named in his honor. In 1967, Hart was named the state's first historic preservation officer, an unpaid position he held until 1978. Hart also

Grave of Joe Holland at Fairmount Cemetery.

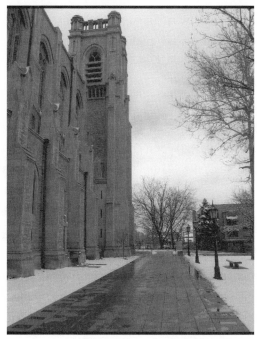

St. John's Walk at St. John's Episcopal Cathedral
in Denver, where Steve Hart is interred.

enjoyed music, and played cello in the Denver Civic Symphony

The two lawyers' skills were highly complementary—with Hart managing much of the traditional corporate practice and Holland being responsible for litigation. Both men, along with Hart's brother Jerry, proved to be good at generating business. The firm rapidly became successful and attracted many corporate clients, but it also reflected their personalities and their desire that the firm be somewhat different from the often stodgy, traditional model of a large, institutional firm. Holland and Hart created an innovative sabbatical program and frequently allowed its lawyers to take on controversial and expensive pro-bono cases, including defending the busing of students in the 1960s and Guantanamo Bay prisoners in 2005.

For the first thirty years of its existence, the firm made its home in the historic Equitable Building at Seventeenth and Stout Streets in downtown Denver. By 1978 some of the partners felt larger and more modern quarters were needed, and—not without controversy or regret—the firm abandoned the Equitable for the thirty-eight-story Anaconda Tower at 555 Seventeenth Street, Denver's tallest building at the time, and since renamed Qwest Tower.

It was also during the 1970s that the firm began to open offices outside of Denver, including those in Aspen, Billings, Boise, Boulder, Cheyenne, Colorado Springs, Denver Tech Center, Jackson, Salt Lake City, and Santa Fe. Although most of the firm's business is regional, it has represented clients from more than thirty countries, and has done significant work in Central and South America.

After his retirement, Holland began spending more time in Palm Springs, and it was there that he died in 1975, at the age of seventy-four. He was buried at Fairmount Cemetery. Hart died at a Denver nursing home eighteen years later, at the age of eighty-five, and his ashes are interred in St. John's Walk at St. John's Episcopal Cathedral in Denver.

$\mathcal{V}$ANCE KIRKLAND
1904–1981

When the new Denver Art Museum opened in 1972 its first exhibition was of the works of Vance Kirkland, who had arrived in Denver in 1929 and remained a dominant force in the art world of Colorado until his death fifty-two years later.

Kirkland was a prolific and hard-working artist who painted from the time he was in high school until, and indeed during, his final hospitalization. He was successful both as an educator and a fiercely independent painter, whose works continue to attract interest and create controversy to this day. Kirkland is represented in many public and private collections throughout the world, including the Art Institute of Chicago, the Smithsonian American Art Museum in Washington, D.C., and several European museums.

He was born in Convoy, Ohio, in 1904. His father was a dentist, and his grandfather had been a doctor, but despite being urged to go into medicine, Kirkland decided at an early age to be an artist. Aware of the challenges of making a living as an artist, Kirkland received degrees from the Cleveland School of Arts in both art and education—figuring that if success as an artist eluded him he could make a living teaching the subject. As it turned out, he did both.

Kirkland arrived in Denver in January 1929, becoming the founding director of the Art School at the University of Denver when he was twenty-four. The previous year he had traveled to the southwest and visited Taos, New Mexico, which was already well known in the art world. However, unlike most artists who came

Vance Kirkland in 1978 at the age of seventy-four. He stands in front of *Explosions of Energy Near the Sun Fifty Billion Years B.C.* at the Denver Art Museum during a fifty-year retrospective of his work.

The Kirkland Museum in Denver. Vance Kirkland's ashes were scattered here and at his nearby home.

West, Kirkland was unimpressed by what he saw in Western art—and particularly the landscape tradition that dated back to Thomas Moran and Albert Bierstadt in the nineteenth century, and continued to dominate Western art. Kirkland found it boring.

Kirkland was influenced more by the European ideas he had picked up from his teachers in Cleveland and on trips to Europe. Upon arriving in Colorado, he embarked on his first and second artistic "periods," characterized by realist—and then by surrealist—watercolors. They presented the West in ways it had seldom been depicted. These works brought Kirkland national attention, and he began a long association with a major New York gallery.

Although Kirkland worked hard as an artist—in his lifetime he turned out more than 1,100 works and 500 drawings—he also created a parallel career as an educator. He directed the University of Denver's (DU) art school from 1929 until 1932, when he resigned after a dispute over the kinds of degrees the university was willing to award art students. He opened his own school at Thirteenth Avenue and Pearl Street in Denver, taking with him many of his former students from DU. In 1933 Kirkland began working closely with the University of Colorado, and an arrangement soon developed whereby his students could get university credit for their art classes, and university students could take art classes—for credit—at the Kirkland School of Art.

In 1941, Kirkland married Anne Oliphant, a librarian who loved art, and who loved Kirkland's work—at least at the time.

Kirkland's career as an educator came full circle in 1946, when he rejoined the University of Denver again as head of the art school and chairman of the arts and humanities department. To persuade Kirkland to return to DU, the school reportedly had to offer him a salary that was higher than that of the chancellor of the university and also had to allow him to report directly to the chancellor, thus enabling him to avoid some of the bickering with other university administrators that had led to his leaving DU fourteen years earlier. Given free rein, Kirkland shifted the school's emphasis from training students how to teach art in elementary schools to becoming practicing artists. For the next twenty-three years he was largely responsible for building the DU art program, one of the university's largest and most successful art departments.

Shortly after returning to the University of Denver, Kirkland made another career change. By the early 1950s, he had become increasingly dissatisfied with his work, despite the fact that his commercial success had never been greater. His New York gallery, Knoedler & Company, told him that there was great demand for his surrealist watercolors, but Kirkland saw only a dead-end. He felt he had exhausted what he could do with that style and resisted the temptation to churn out a profusion of salable, derivative works.

Instead, Kirkland entered his next and most controversial artistic style. He began experimenting with increasingly abstract works and abandoned the smaller medium of watercolors for larger oil and oil-water compositions, sometimes consisting of tens of thousands of small dots applied laboriously with the end of a dowel. He also began to paint interpretations of places he had seen on his international travels, as well as his visions of the universe and abstractions of explosions and energy in space. One later work, for example, was titled *Explosions on a Sun Seventy Billion Light Years from Earth*.

Most critics who had liked Kirkland's earlier work were dismayed—including his New York dealer and even his wife, who apparently never came to the studio after Kirkland's change of style.

Like many artists, Kirkland was opinionated, unconventional, and—at times—cantankerous. He also had a wry, acerbic wit. In 1938 he painted a watercolor based on his observation of the audience at a lecture about wildlife preservation at the Denver Museum of Natural History. The painting portrays the lecture's audience of elegantly dressed society women—all wearing furs! He titled it *Nature Lovers.*

Another time Kirkland was commissioned to paint a mural to hang on the wall of the bar of a wealthy Denver man. He was told the subject of the mural was to be "the seven ages of man." Kirkland found the concept too pretentious for his tastes and painted instead "the seven drinks of man," beginning with mother's milk and ending with embalming fluid.

In 1969 Kirkland became seriously ill with hepatitis and thereafter his health was often poor and work was difficult. His wife died early the next year. His last years were spent trying to maintain a demanding schedule—a minimum of a six-day week at the studio despite the effects of age and illness. Even when he entered the hospital just before his death, he insisted on having painting materials brought in so he could paint from bed, and he was still working on one canvas when he died on Sunday, May 24, 1981. As he wished, no services were held, and his ashes were scattered at his home at 817 Pearl Street and at his nearby studio at Thirteenth Avenue and Pearl—now the Kirkland Museum.

Most of his private art collection, as well as many of his own works, were donated to the Denver Art Museum, where he had served on the board of directors and was the honorary curator of modern art.

Since his death, Kirkland's work has gone through several cycles of being in or out of favor. Due largely to the efforts of Hugh Grant at the Kirkland Museum, his work continues to be discussed, displayed, and sold, and the ultimate judgment of his stature as an artist has yet to be rendered.

Mary Chase at home in Denver with her dog in 1945. *Rocky Mountain News* photo.

ℳ*ARY MCDONOUGH COYLE CHASE*
1906–1981

Pulitzer Prize–winning Mary Chase was born in Denver on February 25, 1906, attended Denver public schools, and graduated from West High School in 1922. Her home, at 532 West Fourth Avenue, has been named an official Denver landmark.

She briefly attended both the University of Denver and the University of Colorado, and although she graduated from neither, she received an honorary Doctor of Literature degree from DU in 1947. When she was eighteen she began working as a reporter for the *Rocky Mountain News,* hired, according to the editor, because of both her writing ability and her shapely legs. Legendary *News* photographer Harry Rhoads worked with Chase—and almost everyone else in Denver journalism in the twentieth century—and recalled her as having been the most attractive woman he had met in his more than seventy years in the newspaper business. But, if her looks apparently had helped her get the job, it was her writing that enabled her to succeed at the paper, eventually moving from reporter to columnist. She married a fellow reporter, and later managing editor, Robert Lamont Chase in 1928.

In the 1930s, Mary Chase left the *News* to combine writing with raising her three children at home, 1376 St. Paul Street. She did freelance writing for United Press and did public relations work for the New Deal's National Youth Administration, a federal agency, and for the Teamsters Union. She also began writing short stories and children's books, but it was as a playwright that she would achieve fame.

She wrote at least fourteen plays from *Me Third* in 1936 to *Cocktails With Mimi* in 1974. In 1939 one of her short stories, *Chi House,* was adapted by Dalton Trumbo, also a Colorado native, for the RKO Pictures movie *Sorority House,* a comedy about a college student's disillusionment with her superficial and elitist sorority sisters.

Although many of Chase's plays were produced, her greatest success by far was 1944's *Harvey,* which ran for 1,775 performances on Broadway. In 1950 it was made into a successful motion picture of the same name starring Jimmy Stewart.

The play, about an imaginary six-foot-one-inch-tall white rabbit, took Chase two years to write. It was inspired, she later said, early one morning during World War II when she looked out her window on a cold, gray day and saw a woman who lived in the neighborhood walking slowly to the bus stop to go to work. She did not know the woman personally, but knew of her. She was a widow who had worked for years to send her only son to college and had learned just a few weeks before that the son had been killed in fighting in the Pacific. Chase recalled wondering at that moment if she could ever write something that would make that woman laugh again. She resolved to try.

Chase drew heavily on the childhood stories of Irish fantasy, super-stition, and folklore relayed to her by her mother, and particularly the story of a pooka—a large horse-like animal that was visible only to the person who believed in it. It was slow going, written mostly at night, while her husband was at the *Rocky Mountain News* that, being a morn-ing paper, required its staff to work evenings. The play went through almost fifty revisions, including a change of name from *The White Rabbit* to *Harvey,* before she sent it off to an agent in New York.

The rest is theater history. *Harvey* opened at the 48th Street Theater with Frank Fay as character Elwood P. Dowd and went on to become one of the longest running plays on Broadway. *Harvey* ran for four and one-half years, grossing almost $10 million, and received the Pulitzer Prize for drama in 1945.

The movie rights to *Harvey* were sold for $1 million, a record amount of money at the time, and the movie featured Jimmy Stewart as the lead. Stewart had first performed the role in 1947, when he filled in on Broadway while Fay was on vacation. Stewart was joined by two members of the Broadway cast: Josephine Hull, who had played the co-starring role of Veta on Broadway, and Jesse White (later to gain even wider fame as the Maytag repairman on television), who played the sanitarium orderly. Stewart was nominated for an Academy Award for the movie, and Josephine Hull won Best Supporting Actress.

Stewart would return to *Harvey* again and again, reprising the role on television and on Broadway in a 1970s revival. Stewart's final appearance as Elwood was in the 1975 London stage version of *Harvey*. The original movie version continues to sell well in the

The Chase gravesite at Crown Hill Cemetery. Note the "Harvey" tombstone in the background. Perhaps a coincidence, perhaps not.

home video and television syndication markets.

Despite the onslaught of fame and publicity, Mary Chase stayed in Denver, continuing to write and raise her family. She donated the originals of her plays to the University of Denver's theater department, where she briefly taught an advanced playwriting class in the 1960s. She wrote nine more plays in the next thirty years, most of them having *Harvey*-like fantasy overtones. Five of her later plays were produced, including, in 1952, the very successful *Mrs. McThing,* a children's comic fantasy starring Helen Hayes. It was originally intended solely as a play for children, but it ran for a year on Broadway and later in London. At the same time another Chase play, *Bernadine,* opened on Broadway. The play, which features an imaginary teenager, was also originally written for children. During these years she also founded the House of Hope, a charitable organization and a home for women with alcohol problems—a project that grew out of her own experience with alcohol and depression, one of the side effects of her rapid rise to fame.

Following the success of *Harvey,* Chase and her family moved from St. Paul Street to a larger house at 505 Circle Drive in Denver's Country Club district. It was there that she suffered a fatal heart attack on October 20, 1981. She is buried at Crown Hill Cemetery in Lakewood. In what is probably just a remarkable coincidence, a few feet behind Chase's grave is a tombstone bearing the name Harvey in large letters. Buried there are Edwin and Doris Harvey who, so far as is known, had no connection to Chase. No one knows how this occurred or what actually happened, although the Chases selected the gravesite in 1974, two years after the Harvey marker was installed. It is possible that Mary Chase—who had a reputation for practical joking—may have noticed the Harvey tombstone and quietly decided on one last practical joke.

ℒ*LOYD J. KING*
1906–1998

Lloyd J. King was born in Kansas on April 21, 1906. He moved to Colorado and entered the grocery business, eventually co-owning five Save-A-Nickel stores, which he sold when he entered the Navy during World War II.

Returning to Denver after the war, King re-entered the grocery business with Chuck Houchens, who would become King's long-time partner and who had worked with King at the Save-A-Nickel stores. Their first store opened at West Colfax Avenue and Vance Street. It was an open-air fruit and vegetable market, which they selected because they couldn't get sufficient building materials for a full grocery due to the post-war shortages. That was followed by an Arvada meat market—which by mid-1947 became the first King Soopers store. Curiously, to this day no one seems to know why King and Houchens decided to spell "Soopers" the way they did.

King bought several smaller groceries before opening his first large supermarket store, at Fourteenth Avenue and Kearney Street in 1951. Later that same year he and his wife, Eleanor, were among the founders of the Bow Mar residential subdivision southwest of Denver.

During the next ten years, King Soopers grew rapidly, adding about a store a year. King was an innovative grocer, an "idea-man," in the words of former King Soopers president Jim Baldwin, who recognized that customers wanted greater control and convenience in their shopping. He understood and liked people and was customer-oriented long before that idea became a cliché. The King Soopers'

Lloyd King, founder of King Soopers.

The King family gravesite at Fairmount
Cemetery.

slogan was "Our people make the difference," and King believed it.

Before World War II, almost all groceries in the United States operated on an "over-the-counter" basis, in which customers would tell the grocer the items they wanted. The grocer would retrieve the items from shelves—most of which were off-limits to customers and required the use by the grocer of a long extension arm to reach items on higher shelves. The process was slow, inconvenient, and inefficient for both employees and customers. King was the first grocer in Colorado—and one of the first in the nation—to introduce such features as a self-service meat department, in which the meat was already cut and packaged in various sizes. The store's butchers could prepare the meat at times when they weren't busy, and customers could grab their pound of ground round without waiting in line.

In 1951 King, with heavy promotional backing from Sperry and Hutchinson's S&H Green Stamps, introduced the concept of trading stamps to the Colorado grocery business. The stamps, which were given to customers with each purchase, could be redeemed for free merchandise. King's promotion launched what S&H calls "the Golden Age" of trading stamps: the 1950s and 1960s. What began as a simple promotion soon escalated into something approaching a craze. Before long, King Soopers and most of its competitors were having "stamp wars," offering double, triple, and even quadruple stamps with each purchase. Safeway, whose president refused to offer stamps, began to lose market share in Denver and fought back by slashing prices, only to have that tactic foiled when the Justice Department charged Safeway with selling below cost and filed an anti-trust suit. Safeway continued to try to fight stamps with legislation, lawsuits, and even offers to buy out the stamp companies. All to no avail. In the end, the Safeway president who had bitterly opposed stamps resigned, and many Safeway stores even began offering their own "Gold Bond" stamps.

King continued to innovate, and in 1952 King Soopers became

the first grocery in the country to have a pharmacy department. In 1957 King Soopers, which was operating ten stores, merged with Dillon Company, of Hutchinson, Kansas, but King remained president until 1972—years in which he would add another thirty stores under the King Soopers and City Market names and introduce new in-store departments, such as bakeries, delicatessens, and photo-finishing. Houchens, who had been general manager of the King Soopers chain before the merger, stayed on with Dillon until his retirement in 1968.

In the 1960s the trading-stamp era was replaced by another marketing approach: discounting. Once again King was in the forefront. His adoption of an aggressive pricing philosophy led to the introduction of discount pricing strategies such as "everyday low pricing" and "unit pricing." In a well-publicized 1968 event, all the King Soopers stores were closed for three days, and their windows were papered over, while employees began marking down prices on virtually all products. The stores reopened as "King Soopers Discount" stores—minus trading stamps. The promotion took King's competitors by surprise and increased King Soopers market share. Later, King was one of the first to offer low-priced, plain-labeled generic products.

King retired in 1972, and in 1983 the Dillon-King Sooper stores were taken over by a national supermarket chain in Cincinnati, which had been founded in 1883 by another grocery pioneer, Barney Kroger. Even during retirement, King usually turned up at the openings of new stores as the company—which is still the largest retailer in the state—continued to expand. In addition to King Soopers and City Market, Kroger operates grocery stores under its own name as well as Ralph's, Smith's and Fry's.

Lloyd King died on January 12, 1998, at the age of ninety-one, and is buried at Fairmount Cemetery. His former partner, Chuck Houchens, died on April 22, 2003, also at the age of ninety-one.

$\mathcal{E}$UGENE DEBS CERVI
1906–1970

For forty years, Gene Cervi was a prominent and colorful Democratic Party activist and newspaperman in Denver, and he is generally credited with creating the weekly business newspaper format. He was also, in the best sense of the words, "a professional troublemaker," a label given to him admiringly in 1988 by Henry Dubroff when he was editor of the *Denver Business Journal.*

Cervi was born in Centralia, Illinois, on September 2, 1906, the son of a coal miner. When Cervi was nine, his family moved to a ranch near Larkspur, Colorado. He attended Colorado College but had to leave school to work—primarily in mining and construction—to help support his large family.

In 1929 he got a job as a reporter with the *Rocky Mountain News,* moving to the *Denver Post* in 1935. Cervi, who was a Roosevelt Democrat and confirmed liberal, was among a group that started the Denver chapter of the Newspaper Guild, a union for newspaper employees.

When World War II broke out, Cervi left the *Post*, becoming the regional director of the federal Office of War Information. When the war ended, Cervi turned to politics as state chairman for the Democrats and worked for mayoral candidate Quigg Newton in his successful campaign against the incumbent, seventy-seven-year-old Ben Stapleton. Stapleton, who was a Democrat like Cervi, had been mayor for more than two decades. His politics, however—including his lack of enthusiasm for Roosevelt's New Deal—were too conser-

Gene Cervi in 1968, editor of the *Rocky Mountain Journal,* forerunner of the *Denver Business Journal.*
COURTESY OF THE COLORADO HISTORICAL SOCIETY, 93.167.81.

Gene Cervi's tombstone at Mount Olivet Cemetery.

vative for Cervi. In the 1947 election, Stapleton was overwhelmingly defeated by the thirty-five-year-old Newton, who received the backing of both newspapers and a strong coalition of liberal Democrats and moderate Republicans.

Cervi's other post-war venture was writing a four-page newsletter, *Cervi's News Service,* which he began publishing in 1945. The newsletter provided Cervi with an opportunity to develop into a kind journalistic Don Quixote—attacking establishment windmills such as the utility companies, the daily newspapers, and most politicians, including—eventually—Newton. Cervi, never entirely comfortable with too close an association with officeholders, broke with Newton shortly after the election. He also decided to strike out on his own and challenge an old foe, incumbent fellow Democrat Ed Johnson, for the U.S. Senate. Johnson, who had once called Cervi "the worst state chairman in the United States," defeated Cervi in the 1948 primary by more than two to one, carrying every county in the state.

Cervi remained an active Democrat until his death. In the words of *Rocky Mountain News* columnist Gene Amole he was "the 'stormy petrel' of Democratic Party politics." The defeat in his campaign for the senate gave Cervi the opportunity to turn more of his attention back to journalism. In 1949 he converted *Cervi's News Service* to a weekly tabloid: *Cervi's Rocky Mountain Journal.* The *Journal,* while filling the role of a business paper, also provided Cervi with a forum for his views on government, politics, finance, journalism, and anything else that interested him—views which Cervi willingly shared every week. The result was an uneasy but compelling hybrid of business news and liberal investigative journalism, which was must-reading for thousands of people each week. Cervi's journalistic career was perhaps best described by the late Sam Lusky, a friend and former city editor at the *Rocky Mountain News,* who wrote that in his days as a miner, Cervi set "dynamite charges which disgorged vast chunks of flying debris from Colorado hillsides, a practice which

Cervi has continued without interruption, at least in the figurative sense, during his newspaper career."

Perhaps more significantly, the *Journal* also served as the pioneer of a new kind of newspaper: the urban weekly business paper. *The Denver Business Journal* is the local descendant of Cervi's *Journal,* but similar publications now exist in most major cities—and many smaller ones—in the world. Shortly after his death, the International Society of Weekly Newspaper Editors created the Eugene Cervi Award, given annually to an editor in recognition of a career of community journalism, notably including a record of "aggressive reporting of government at the grassroots level."

Cervi remained active in politics and the *Journal* into his sixties, although day-to-day operations passed to his daughter, Clé. He died of a heart attack on December 15, 1970 at the age of sixty-four, and is buried at Mt. Olivet Cemetery in Denver.

ELREY BORGE JEPPESEN
1907–1996

The main terminal at Denver International Airport is named after one of aviation's true pioneers—a man whose first pilot's license, in 1923, was signed by Orville Wright.

Elrey "Captain Jepp" Jeppesen was born on January 28, 1907, in the town of Lake Charles in western Louisiana. He grew up in Hood River, Oregon, in the 1920s—a time when aviation was still in its infancy but was taking the world by storm. Pilots were among the heroes of the day, and flying shows and flying circuses were hugely popular public attractions.

When Jeppesen was fourteen years old, he took his first ride in an airplane, and two years later he quit high school, got a pilot's license, and bought a war-surplus Curtiss JN-4 "Jenny" biplane for $500. The JN-4 had been the Army's primary training aircraft during World War I and remained popular with stunt pilots and barnstormers into the 1930s. It was a versatile, maneuverable aircraft, with a top speed of about 75 miles per hour—not fast by today's standards, but faster than most cars of its era.

Jeppesen's aviation career took him from Tex Rankin's Flying Circus in Portland, Oregon, to Fairchild Aerial Surveys, then to Varney Airlines and Boeing Air Transport, working as a mail pilot flying between Cheyenne, Wyoming, and Oakland, California, one of the most hazardous routes at that time. Jeppesen's airplane was a Boeing 40B, an open-cockpit biplane, which could carry about 1,200 pounds of mail at speeds up to 130 miles an hour. In the late

"Captain Jepp" in an early United Airlines photo.

The grave of "Jepp" Jeppesen and his wife, Nadine,
at Fairmount Cemetery.

1930s Varney and Boeing Air Transport merged to form United Airlines, and Jeppesen became a United pilot. It was at United that Jeppesen met his wife, Nadine, who was one of the airline's first flight attendants. They made their home in Salt Lake City.

In the early days of aviation, navigation was done from memory or with the aid of automobile road maps and by following railroad tracks. Jeppesen had not been flying long before he began keeping his own small black loose-leaf notebook of navigational charts and maps, carefully noting elevations and the locations of landmarks and obstructions, including landing strips, beacons, water towers, and smokestacks. When he was unable to get information about an object from other sources, he would personally strap an altimeter on his back, and climb the object to determine its height. It was a tedious and painstaking process, and Jeppesen once remarked to a reporter: "People say it's a small world. They ought to try charting it!"

What started as a hobby began to grow into a business in the 1930s. He sold a copy of his "Little Black Book" to a fellow pilot in 1934, and by 1936 he and his wife were operating a home-based chart business out of their basement.

In 1941 Jeppesen moved to Denver, still working as a United pilot. By this time the *Jeppesen Airway Manual* had come a long way from the little handwritten book. Jeppesen and his employees had charted most of the important air routes of the United States, and the books, often called "Jepp charts," were becoming standard equipment for private, commercial, and military pilots. He also began producing products for radio and instrument navigation, and introduced the first instrument approach charts. The business outgrew Jeppesen's Denver home and was moved into a nearby commercial building.

Following World War II, the growth of aviation was rapid. What had been a curious and exotic business in the 1930s moved into the mainstream in the late 1940s. Most of the airlines adopted Jeppesen's charts, as did the Air Force. The business expanded rapidly, and in 1954, when Jeppesen retired as a United pilot, he was running a large and successful company, which dominated the air navigation business.

In 1961 Jeppesen sold the business to Times-Mirror Publishing Company, although he continued to run it until 1988, by which time paper manuals and radio-based systems largely had been replaced by computerized products. The company, by then called Jeppesen Sanderson, was the world's leading publisher of both air navigational information and flight training systems.

Jeppesen died at his home in Cherry Hills Village, Colorado, on November 26, 1996 at the age of eighty-nine, and is buried at Fairmount Cemetery. He did not live to see the day in October 2000 when the company he founded was acquired by Boeing Corporation, the world's largest aerospace company and—coincidentally—the original owner of Boeing Air Transport, the company that sixty-five years earlier had employed him as a mail pilot. Jeppesen's headquarters are still in Englewood, Colorado, but it has offices as far away as China and Australia. The company has more than 1,400 employees.

In 1997 Jeppesen's extensive collection of aeronautical memorabilia, including the hand-drawn charts that made up his first Little Black Books, was given to the Museum of Flight in Seattle. Jeppesen's early flying career is featured in the Microsoft computer video game *Flight Simulator 2004: A Century of Flight,* which simulates an early mail flight from Cheyenne, Wyoming, to Salt Lake City, Utah. Microsoft tells players that "in the spirit of Elrey Jeppesen, this Flight challenges you to get the mail to where it needs to go."

$\mathcal{J}$AMES QUIGG NEWTON, JR.
1911–2003

In 1947 most people in Colorado were stunned at the election of "Boy Mayor" Quigg Newton, a thirty-five-year-old newcomer to politics. Newton had—somehow—defeated Ben Stapleton, the seventy-seven-year-old incumbent who had been elected mayor five times and had first been elected twenty-four years earlier in 1923. In fact, the roots of Stapleton's political organization went back even further, to the administration of Stapleton's mentor, Mayor Robert Speer, who had first been elected in 1904.

As with many mayors who stay in office for a long time, Stapleton was vulnerable to charges of cronyism and association with a political "machine." On a larger scale, Denver was faced with postwar challenges and pressures, which voters apparently believed would be handled better by a younger man with fresh ideas.

Although Newton was certainly young and may have had fresh ideas, he was no more an outsider than Stapleton had been. He was a Denver native, the son of a wealthy Denver businessman, and was married to Virginia Shafroth, whose grandfather had been a United States senator from Colorado, and had also served as governor from 1909 to 1913. After graduating from law school at Yale and working for a year with William O. Douglas, then head of the Securities and Exchange Commission, Newton returned to Denver in 1937 and joined Lewis and Grant, one of Denver's most prominent law firms. Already at the firm was Richard Davis, a Yale classmate who had married Newton's sister, Nancy, in 1935. In 1938 Newton and Davis left

A new generation in Denver politics. Outgoing long-
time Mayor Ben Stapleton poses with his successor,
Quigg Newton, as they look at the city from a window
in the mayor's office in the City and County Building.
COURTESY OF THE COLORADO HISTORICAL SOCIETY, F38961.

the firm to open their own law office. Because of their familiarity with the increasingly important areas of tax and regulatory law their firm prospered.

Newton's private law practice was interrupted by World War II, when he served as a legal officer in the United States Navy. Shortly after his return to Denver in 1946, Newton attended a breakfast for his former employer William O. Douglas, by then a justice of the Supreme Court. The breakfast was held at the Brown Palace apartment of E. Palmer "Ep" Hoyt, editor and publisher of the *Denver Post* and an outspoken opponent of Mayor Stapleton. Everyone was surprised when, following Hoyt's remark that he was hoping an attractive candidate could be found to run against Stapleton in the 1947 election, Douglas said "What about Quigg?" Up until that time, Newton had not been particularly interested in partisan politics and was not even a member of a political party.

In the absence of any candidates who appealed to him, Hoyt convinced Newton to run, with the implied backing of the *Denver Post*. The election was a three-way race, with Newton, running as an independent with some strong Republican ties, facing Stapleton and former U.S. Attorney Tom Morrissey—both Democrats. Whether because of his age, or his dislike for campaigning, Stapleton ran a weak race against Newton, who had put together a coalition of Republicans and "reform" Democrats. Newton's campaign also appealed to thousands of new voters who had arrived in Denver since the war—primarily ex-servicemen and women who had been stationed in Colorado during the war and grew to like it. Newton appeared to be comfortable with the postwar changes that were taking place in Denver, while Stapleton seemed to yearn for the past, and Morrissey's campaign never really found a voice or a theme.

When the dust cleared in May of 1947, everyone was astounded by the enormity of Newton's victory. He received almost 58 percent of the vote, Morrissey just 25 percent, and Stapleton a humiliating 12 percent. The repudiation of the old guard was complete, and Denver had elected the youngest mayor in its history.

Newton served two terms and oversaw the change of Denver from a small, quiet city to a fast-growing, fast-changing one. There was scarcely any area of city government that was not changed during Newton's terms in office, including introducing a Career Service Authority to replace the old political patronage system, establishing competitive bidding for city contracts, beginning what would eventually become the Denver Regional Council of Governments, creating the first Community Relations Commission and, with Dr. Florence Rena Sabin, reforming and updating the city's health department.

Denver also embarked on a building boom that transformed the face of the city—for better or worse. Among projects completed during Newton's tenure in office were the Coliseum, the Botanic Gardens, the downtown public library, the city auditorium, more than 2,000 public housing units, major expansions of the airport and the Museum of Natural History (now Nature and Science), and many road projects—including the Valley Highway (now Interstate 25), one-way streets, and new parking lots to accommodate the post-war growth of automobile travel.

In July 1953 Newton registered as a Democrat so that he would be able to run for the U.S. Senate seat that was being vacated by "Big Ed" Johnson, a conservative Democrat. However, Newton's senate bid ran into strong opposition from the organized labor wing of the party, and he was defeated in the statewide primary—and even in the Denver precincts—by John Carroll, who in turn lost the general election to Republican Gordon Allott. Newton returned to City Hall, but his enthusiasm for electoral politics was diminished and he would never run again.

By 1955 Newton's job as mayor had ceased being enjoyable. He had suffered losses on several key bond issues and reform proposals, and the city faced a severe drought that threatened to slow down development. He declined to run for reelection, and by mid-1955, newly out of office after eight years, he had abandoned both politics and Denver itself to move to New York as vice president of the Ford Foundation.

His absence was brief, however, and in 1956 he returned to the state as president of the University of Colorado. Still a young man, at the age of forty-five, Newton's seven-year tenure at the university was an active and sometimes stormy one. He succeeded in attracting several prominent research programs and faculty members, and his building agenda expanded the east side of the campus and mandated the uniform use of the distinctive earth-tone stonework and red tile roof designs that characterize much of the campus to this day.

Denver's "boy" mayor, Quigg Newton, is buried at his family gravesite at Fairmount Cemetery.

But he also became embroiled in ongoing budget disputes with the fiscally conservative state legislature and got enmeshed in several highly public battles, including a fight over the political bias of the school's newspaper and the unpopular firing of Everett "Sonny" Grandelius. Grandelius, CU's controversial but successful football coach, led Colorado to national prominence and the Orange Bowl in the 1961–62 season with a 9–2 record. However, an NCAA investigation targeted Grandelius, and Newton fired him. The next year, under Grandelius's successor, CU fell to 2–8, and most of the losses were by lopsided scores, including consecutive losses to Oklahoma and Missouri by scores of 62–0 and 57–0. Many fans and alumni blamed Newton rather than Grandelius's off-field management, which, according to the NCAA, included running a "slush fund" for making payments to players. The NCAA placed CU on two years' probation, and many players from the 1961 team were forced to quit. In 1963 Newton returned again to the quieter world of foundations, first in New York and then in California.

Finally, in 1981, Newton came back to Colorado at the age of seventy to rejoin his former law partner and brother-in-law, Richard Davis, who by then headed one of Denver's leading law firms: Davis, Graham, and Stubbs. Newton continued to practice law with the firm until his death of a heart attack on April 4, 2003. He is buried in a family plot at Fairmount Cemetery.

$\mathscr{B}$YRON RAYMOND WHITE
1917–2002

When he died in 2002, the *Rocky Mountain News* front page story about retired United States Supreme Court Justice Byron White began with the sub-headline: "Colorado's Superman led life of effortless excellence." It was only a slight exaggeration.

From his birth in Ft. Collins in 1917 to his death in Denver eighty-five years later, White was that rare kind of individual: a supreme achiever and a genuinely and deeply reserved person. It was ironic that the quiet White would forever be known to the world by the flamboyant and unlikely nickname "Whizzer." Denver sportswriter Leonard Cahn gave White this name because of his speed on the field when he was an All-American running back at the University of Colorado. To White's dismay, the nickname stuck.

Although White was born in Ft. Collins, he grew up in the nearby small town of Wellington, where he worked as a child alongside his older brother, Sam, picking sugar beets during harvest and helping out at his father's small lumberyard. In 1934 he graduated from Wellington High School, where he was a star athlete in football, basketball, and baseball and was the class valedictorian. That same year he entered the University of Colorado on an academic scholarship. Once again he excelled. In sports he played baseball, earned all-conference honors as a guard on the basketball team, and in 1937 he was named an All-American player while leading the undefeated Colorado football team to the Cotton Bowl. That year he led the nation in rushing and scoring. His academic career was equally

Byron White.

Future Supreme Court Justice **Byron "Whizzer" White** runs for a
long gain for the University of Colorado against Rice University in the
1938 Cotton Bowl in Dallas. White not only played offense and
defense, but he also kicked extra points. He was named most valuable
player in the game, even though Rice won 28-14.

notable, including graduating first in his class and being awarded a Rhodes Scholarship to Oxford University.

After graduating from Colorado, White, by then reluctantly carrying the nickname "Whizzer," received a National Football League contract that made him the highest paid football player of his day, earning twice what was paid to the next highest-paid star, quarterback and eventual Pro-Football Hall-of-Famer "Slingin' Sammy" Baugh of the Washington Redskins. White spent the next few years balancing playing football with studying at Oxford—where his path first, and briefly, crossed that of John F. Kennedy, whose father was United States Ambassador to Great Britain. White then entered Yale Law School, continuing to follow two seemingly incompatible careers. With the Detroit Lions in 1940, he led the NFL in rushing, while at Yale he was, as he had been at Colorado, first in his class.

World War II ended his NFL career, and White became an intelligence officer in the navy, where he again met Kennedy, and the two became friends while both were serving in the Pacific. In the navy White earned two bronze stars for bravery in battle, including helping defend two aircraft carriers against Japanese kamikaze attacks.

In 1946 White returned to civilian life, graduating from Yale Law School—first in his class—and marrying Marion Stearns, whom he had met in college and whose father had been president of the University of Colorado. After clerking in Washington, D.C. for the Chief Justice of the United States Supreme Court, White returned to Denver in 1947 and joined the law firm of Lewis, Grant, and Davis. He spent the next thirteen years in Denver, practicing law and raising his family.

Meanwhile, his ex-navy friend, John Kennedy, was climbing the political ladder and had been elected to Congress from Massachusetts. The two had stayed in touch and in 1958, when Kennedy decided to run for the presidency, he called on White for help. While still practicing law in Denver, White began working with the Kennedy campaign—first heading the effort in Colorado and then becoming co-chairman of the national campaign.

After Kennedy's election as president in 1960, White became deputy U.S. attorney general under Robert Kennedy, the President's brother. White's short career at the Justice Department was marked by his efforts to protect civil rights workers in the south, in the face of determined, and often violent, opposition. In 1962, in a surprise move, President Kennedy nominated White to the Supreme Court.

White's career on the Court was both long—thirty-one years—and somewhat controversial. Although he was a registered Democrat, apparently no one in the Kennedy administration had ever taken the time to find out much about his political philosophy. Nor were his views examined closely when he went before the Senate for confirmation. His nomination sailed through the Democrat-controlled Senate on a voice vote after just one brief, ninety-minute hearing, in which the questioning was deferential and perfunctory.

On the bench, White proved to be far more traditional, conservative, and law-and-order-oriented than the Democrats had expected. In this he was a reverse image of the chief justice at the time, Earl Warren. Warren was a moderate Republican who had been appointed by fellow Republican Dwight Eisenhower in 1953. Eisenhower hoped that, based on his record as a tough prosecutor in California, Warren would bring a more conservative voice to a court dominated by the liberal judges appointed by Democrats Franklin D. Roosevelt and Harry Truman. Warren not only turned out to be more liberal than expected, but he was also considered a judicial activist, under whom the Court soon became known as the "Warren Court" and gained a reputation as one of the most liberal and proactive courts in history.

White quickly became one of the few dissenting voices on the Warren Court. He was a judicial traditionalist who believed the

Court's job involved a strict interpretation of the Constitution, and he had an aversion for the Warren Court's fondness for, as White saw it, making law.

In case after case, including such landmarks as *Roe v. Wade*—which established a constitutional right to legal abortion—and *Miranda v. Arizona*—which gave new rights to suspects in criminal cases, White dissented. Over the course of his thirty-one-year career, White remained a strict constitutionalist, holding to a strong belief that it was up to elected officials, not appointed judges, to make or change laws.

After Warren retired in 1969, the Court gradually began to lose some of its liberal, activist orientation, and in White's remaining twenty-five years on the bench he was more often a member of the

Justice Byron White's ashes are interred on the west side of the All Soul's Walk at St. John's Episcopal Cathedral in Denver.

Court's majority and less often the lone or lonely dissenter. He was considered to be a moderating influence on those to the right and left of him, and a leader of the effort to make sure the Court's procedures and decisions were consistent with sound legal principals.

He was also regarded as an austere presence on the bench and a very tough interrogator of lawyers appearing before the Court.

White had always been disdainful of the press and of publicity—a feeling that some traced back to his days as a football player when he disliked some of the coverage he received in the press—perhaps including the unwelcome nickname he had been given. Whatever the cause, White was generally reserved and aloof around the press and public. Unlike some of his fellow justices, who sought publicity and forums for expressing their private views on public issues, White stayed in the background, playing an influential but low-profile role on the Court.

Following his retirement from the Court in 1993, White split his time between his home in McLean, Virginia, and Denver, Colorado, where, in 1994 the Federal Courthouse was named in his honor. He died in Denver in 2002 from complications of pneumonia. For a man who shunned pomp and publicity, his funeral at St. John's Cathedral in Denver was an anomaly. It was one of the largest and most publicized funerals ever conducted in Colorado—perhaps rivaled only by the ceremony for William F. "Buffalo Bill" Cody. More than a thousand people attended, including five fellow justices of the Supreme Court and scores of political figures, including Senator Edward Kennedy from Massachusetts, and Ethel Kennedy, widow of Robert Kennedy. White's ashes were interred in All Souls Walk at St. John's Cathedral.

$\mathcal{B}$ILL DANIELS
1920–2000

In 1948 the most-coveted Christmas item was a new invention called television—broadcast from a handful of stations around the country to an only slightly larger handful of black-and-white television sets with screens that ranged in size from three to twelve inches and cost almost three months' salary for the average worker. In that same year, there began a revolution in the way television would be distributed. An appliance storeowner in rural Arkansas put up a tower to receive television signals from a station in Memphis, Tennessee. The signals were displayed on the television sets in his store—which would otherwise have been blank—and were also sent to a nearby home where one of the store's customers paid $3 a month to get the Memphis signal.

Such were the humble beginnings of something called "community antenna systems" or CATV, which were created by entrepreneurs to bring distant television signals to rural and mountainous communities where there were no other sources of programming.

Four years later, Bill Daniels, a thirty-two-year-old insurance salesman from Casper, Wyoming, was sitting in a Denver bar watching a boxing match. Daniels loved boxing, and had won two Golden Gloves championships in New Mexico, where his family had moved from his birthplace in Greeley, Colorado. Educated at New Mexico Military Institute, Daniels had flown fighter jets in World War II and the Korean War and with the Navy's Blue Angels high performance team. By 1952 he was released from active service, and was already

Bill Daniels at his Denver headquarters.
COURTESY OF THE DANIELS FUND.

getting bored with the insurance business in Wyoming. He also thought it was unfair that people in Wyoming didn't have access to television.

When he returned to Casper, Daniels decided to do something about it, and he started a small community antenna system to pick up the television signal from Denver's Channel 2 and redistribute it to the residents of Casper. His first system had only single-channel capacity, so as soon as Denver had more than one television station Daniels began polling his subscribers in Casper every few months to find out which station they wanted to watch.

The scenario was being repeated in rural areas all around the country as entrepreneurs erected towers, strung cable, and began pocketing $5 a month or so from television-starved subscribers. It seemed like a good, if unspectacular, business. But some people believed competition—either from the phone companies or from the licensing of more television stations in smaller and rural areas—might put an end to the need for CATV.

Daniels saw things differently. He took the business seriously, and foresaw more potential than most of his contemporaries. He pioneered in the use of microwave, which enabled systems to receive more television signals than were possible with single towers. He moved his business to Denver in 1955, began buying out small CATV systems and helped create the National Cable Television Association, a highly successful industry trade association which lobbied at both state and federal levels for favorable legislative and administrative treatment for cable operators. In 1958 he started an investment banking and brokerage business—Daniels & Associates—which eventually grew to be the biggest in the cable industry, and expanded to include other communications businesses, including broadcast stations and telephone companies.

Over the years Daniels sold most of his cable systems while building the brokerage business, a formula that enabled him to become one of the United States' wealthiest individuals by the

1990s—with a net worth of over $1 billion. In the process he also had an enormous impact on Denver's economy. Because of Daniels's choice of Denver as his headquarters, and his prominence within the industry, Denver became the hub for the cable industry during the 1970s and 1980s. Many large and small cable operators and affiliated companies either headquartered in Denver or established a substantial presence in the city.

Daniels's business success gave him the freedom to pursue other interests, initially primarily in the worlds of sports and politics, but eventually in education and philanthropy.

He owned all or part of several sports teams, including basketball's Los Angeles Lakers and, less successfully, the Utah Stars of the old American Basketball Association. He also founded a sports television network, backed a heavyweight boxer's career, was active in auto racing, and helped Denver land a major league baseball team. In politics, Daniels was an active Republican, supporting both individual candidates, such as Ronald Reagan, and conservative causes, such as public school vouchers. His one try for elective office was an unsuccessful race for the Republican nomination for governor of Colorado in 1974, losing to the incumbent, John Vanderhoof, who in turn lost the general election to Dick Lamm.

By the mid-1980s Daniels had passed the traditional retirement age of 65 and began to adjust his priorities. Although he began spending more time in California, where he owned a home and a cable system in Carlsbad, he also turned his attention to what he saw as the needs of Denver. He had been involved in charitable activities all along, including drug-treatment programs and Junior Achievement, but in the 1980s he stepped up his commitment. He founded the Denver's Young Americans Bank in 1987, based on his faith in capitalism and his belief that existing approaches to the business and financial education of children were largely ineffective, if not non-existent. He also decided to leave most of his fortune to a new charity called The Daniels Fund, which, with approximately $1 billion in assets, is Colorado's largest charitable organization. The Fund is dedicated to programs for the benefit of individuals and non-profit organizations in Colorado, Utah, New Mexico, and Wyoming, with a major commitment to providing college scholarships to students.

In the 1980s Daniels began a productive association with the University of Denver—eventually donating millions of dollars and much of his time to the graduate school of business—which would become the Daniels College of Business in 1994.

Long before the accounting and corporate greed scandals of 2001–2002, Daniels was urging the DU business school and others to emphasize responsibility and ethics. This was consistent with Daniels's career as a businessman, where he practiced what he preached.

Bill Daniels's ashes were scattered in the sea near his home in Carlsbad, California.
COURTESY OF JOSH COOPER.

For example, whenever he would complete a successful sale of a business, he would make sure his employees—from top to bottom—received a generous share of profits that he might legally have claimed for himself. Today, many Denver millionaires owe their good fortune to their association with Daniels.

Even more striking were Daniels actions in connection with his ownership of the Utah Stars. The team was successful on the court, winning the league championship in 1971 and making the playoffs almost every year. But the bidding war with the more entrenched National Basketball Association proved too costly for Daniels—who had spent a large sum of money financing his failed gubernatorial bid in 1974. In 1975 the Stars filed for bankruptcy, and the following year the league folded.

Yet Daniels not only managed to pay off all secured creditors but also sought out unsecured creditors such as the team's season ticket holders. He made full restitution, with eight-percent interest, to every ticket holder he could find. As for those he couldn't find, Daniels calculated the amount he owed them and then donated that amount to Utah charities. Despite the demise of the Stars, Daniels remained so popular with Utah fans that he was one of the first members elected to the Utah Basketball Hall of Fame.

As Daniels's obituary in the *Denver Post* noted, he lived as hard as he worked. His lifestyle—which included four marriages—was characterized by rising early, staying up late, and a fondness for cigarettes and alcohol. By the late 1990s his health was declining, and on March 7, 2000, he died at the age of seventy-nine of respiratory failure in a hospital in Rancho Mirage, California. At his request, his ashes were scattered in the ocean near his California home.

$\mathscr{F}$RANK EUGENE AMOLE, JR.
1923–2002

For more than a quarter of a century, until his death in 2002, the voice and the words of Gene Amole represented the start of the day for many Coloradans, first with his morning classical radio program on KVOD and then in his highly personal and very popular column in the *Rocky Mountain News*. So it was with great dismay when, in October 2001, readers turned to Amole's column and read the words "I am dying."

What followed over the next seven months was an extraordinary journalistic good-bye from Amole, who devoted most of his remaining columns to candid accounts of his illness and his effort to die with dignity. In return, the people of Denver delivered their own good-bye to Amole in the form of thousands of letters and phone calls, as well as tributes not normally accorded to newspaper columnists. A portion of Elati Street, near the *Rocky Mountain News* office on West Colfax Avenue in downtown Denver, was renamed by the city as "Gene Amole Way." And after his death, a public ceremony honoring Amole was held at the Civic Center.

Amole was born in Denver on May 24, 1923, and graduated from South High School in 1941. He enrolled at the University of Colorado, but left school after a few months and got a job as a bellhop at a Denver hotel. It was there that he may have gotten the idea of going into radio as a career, reportedly after a guest of the hotel heard Amole paging someone in the lobby and told him that he had such a good voice that he should consider a career in broadcasting.

Gene Amole in 1983 after his final broadcast at the KVOD studio on Ruby Hill, overlooking the lights of Denver. *Rocky Mountain News* file photo, December 1983.
COURTESY OF THE *ROCKY MOUNTAIN NEWS.*

Gravesite of Sergeant Frank "Gene" Amole at Ft. Logan National Cemetery.

He soon got a job as a night announcer at Denver radio station KMYR. The United States had just entered World War II, and in 1942 Amole was drafted. He served in the U.S. Army in Europe with an armored division in General George Patton's 3rd Army, an experience that he frequently wrote about and that left a strong impression on him.

After the war, Amole returned to Denver and resumed his radio career at KMYR, where he hosted a "man on the street" program and became news director. During the Korean War in the early 1950s he became a war correspondent for the *Denver Post* and the Mutual Broadcasting System. Upon his return to Denver, he resumed his local radio career and also began doing television with Channel 2, Denver's first—and at the time only—television station. Television was booming in the early 1950s, and Amole tried to capitalize on it by acquiring the television broadcast license for the new Channel 4; he lost to a politically well-positioned group that included Denver Mayor Quigg Newton, businessman and prominent Democrat Bill Grant, and movie star Bob Hope.

In 1956, Amole and partner Ed Koepke started their own radio station, KDEN-AM, which featured an eclectic programming line-up, including classical music in the evenings and rock music during the day. In 1957, Amole and Koepke added an FM station, KDEN-FM, which later became KVOD-FM, creating what eventually became one of the nation's most successful commercial classical music stations, after first struggling with a more traditional "beautiful music" format (soft popular music).

The highlight of KVOD's classical format, artistically and commercially, was Amole's own morning show, "Music for a New Day," which set the tone for the station's unique personality. Unlike virtually all other classical stations, which sounded stuffy and pretentious, Amole's show at KVOD was breezy, warm and amusing. Amole used to say that although the music was serious, the announcers didn't have to be.

KVOD attracted a very loyal, high-income, well-educated audience who loved Amole's unconventional approach. For example, one of the signatures of Amole's show was his habit of putting a microphone outside KVOD's Ruby Hill studio in west Denver so that listeners could hear the chirping of the birds at the station's feeder in the background as Brahms or Beethoven or a commercial played in the foreground.

Meanwhile, KDEN-AM evolved an unusual and well-executed jazz format, which attracted a small but loyal audience and proved successful in the late 1960s. The station was sold in 1971, and KVOD was sold in 1983. Amole's last show was in December of that year.

In 1977, at the age of fifty-four, Amole was approached by *Rocky Mountain News* editor Michael Balfe Howard to write an opinion column. Howard promised Amole the freedom to write whatever came into his mind, and for the next twenty-five years Amole did just that, three times a week, creating what soon became the paper's most popular feature.

It turned out that as good as Amole had been at broadcasting, writing was his true calling, and the accomplishment for which he is most remembered. As with his radio shows, Amole's column managed to apply an affable and easygoing approach to often serious and controversial topics. Although many disagreed with Amole over the years—one of his first columns was a scathing indictment of a city agency run by a man who was, unknown to Amole, a very close friend of Michael Howard's—few took it personally or attacked Amole. So popular were his columns that they were republished in three successful books: *Morning, Amole Again,* and *Amole One More Time.*

One of the most appealing aspects of Amole's columns was their unpredictability. His choice of subjects ran the gamut, and readers were as likely to read his opinion about Denver's old streetcar system (he loved it) to his opinion of Denver's new airport (he hated it). The public adored his willingness to take on the rich, the popular, and the powerful when he felt it was necessary. The target could be Broncos owner Pat Bowlen, Coors Field, light rail, or the mayor. Amole always wrote it as he saw it, but also wrote it with his distinctive wit and humility, somehow softening the blow.

It was in October 2001 that Amole revealed in his column his impending death. The news wasn't entirely unexpected; he had been ill for some time. Still, it came as a shock to read, "I finally reached the point where I realized there is no cure for the many ailments nibbling away at what is left of my life." From that time until May of the following year, Amole shared with readers—in his usual unique way—his thoughts and feelings as he approached death. Once again, the subject matter was serious, but Amole's treatment of it was never gloomy, maudlin, or self-pitying.

His last column appeared on the front page of the *News* on the morning of Monday, May 13, 2002. He had died the previous afternoon at the age of seventy-eight, at home and with his wife, Patricia, and family. It was vintage Amole: unpretentious and grateful, not ponderous or inflated with self-importance.

> *I . . . hope that along the way I have said, written or spoken something of value to those who survive me. Certainly I make no claim of original thought, but perhaps I have taken an existing idea and added something of value to it. You are a better judge of that than I.*
>
> *I was privileged to spend many of my last years at this proud old newspaper. To work here and become a part of its legacy was a great gift to me.*
>
> *Now, I'm gone.*
> *Goodbye*

Amole was buried at Ft. Logan National Cemetery.

William Berger and his collection at the Denver Art Museum.
COURTESY OF THE DENVER ART MUSEUM.

William Berger family gravesite, Fairmount Cemetery.

$\mathcal{W}$ILLIAM MERRIAM BART BERGER
1925–1999

The fact that Denver has been the home to many mutual fund businesses is due largely to people such as Bill Berger. Berger was to the city's mutual fund business what Bill Daniels was to its cable businesses: a pioneer and a patriarch.

Berger was born in Denver on November 3, 1925. He graduated from Yale, where he majored in English, after interrupting his education to serve as an ambulance driver for the British Eighth Army during World War II. Returning to Denver, Berger began managing money at Colorado National Bank, which had been started by one of Berger's great-grandfathers in 1862.

Berger became involved with mutual funds through the Centennial Management Company, one of the first tax-free exchange funds, which permitted investors to exchange shares of stock owned by them for stock in a mutual fund without incurring any tax liability.

Before starting his own Berger Funds in 1974, Berger was involved in the establishment of both Founders Funds and Financial Programs, now AIM/Invesco, and for a time in the 1960s, he shared office space with Tom Bailey, who would go on to start Janus Funds. For twenty years Berger headed and managed the successful Berger 100 and Berger 101 funds. In 1990 Berger, then sixty-five, delegated most day-to-day portfolio management operations to an associate, and in 1994 he sold a majority interest in his company to Kansas City Southern Industries. Even after the sale, Berger continued as he had before, appearing frequently in television ads for Berger Funds and being interviewed by financial journalists. He was effective on television—a familiar and easily recognizable figure, standing more than six feet, four inches tall and, in later life, sporting a white beard. Berger's distinctive and forceful public image helped people remember and identify with his funds. Along with John Bogle of the much larger Vanguard Funds, he was one of the most well-known spokesmen for no-load mutual funds during the 1980s and 1990s.

In 2000 Kansas City Southern, which had also acquired Denver-based Janus Funds, spun off both companies into Stilwell Financial. Berger Funds continued to operate as an independent subsidiary at Second and University in the Cherry Creek area of Denver, managing twelve mutual funds with more than $15 billion in assets. However, Berger's core growth funds were not performing well, and the style of investing that was followed by many Berger and Janus funds was hit particularly hard by the bear market that began in 2000. In an effort to improve profitability and performance, Stillwell decided in 2002 to consolidate all its funds under the Janus name—a move that not only eliminated Berger Funds as an independent Stillwell subsidiary and closed or consolidated the thirteen Berger funds, but also removed the Berger name itself from the mutual funds business. Janus Funds is the surviving, publicly traded company, still based in the Cherry Creek area of Denver.

After Berger had sold his funds, he and his wife, Bernadette, increasingly focused their energies on completing a major English art collection. Berger also worked hard on behalf of the Denver Art Museum and its efforts to expand in the mid-1990s, and he started the Berger Collection Educational Trust. The Berger Collection found a permanent home at the museum, and British pieces ranging from the 1500s to today are featured on the sixth floor.

Berger believed that creating an art collection required many of the same qualities he found useful in building and managing a portfolio of stocks—including negotiation, evaluation, and timing. If Berger's stock selection was sometimes contrarian, seeking bargains where few others found it, so too in buying British art he chose what many considered to be an "undervalued" area. Notwithstanding the greater reputation of French, Italian, and Dutch artists, the Bergers chose to build their collection based on their fondness for Britain and their strong interest in and support of British culture. Art critics speculate that the existence of the Berger collection, and the Berger Collection Educational Trust, may help further popularize British art, much as has occurred since the founding in 1977 of the Yale Center for British Art by another financier and an earlier Yale graduate, Paul Mellon, class of 1929. The Berger Trust, in cooperation with *The British Art Journal,* makes annual awards for achievements in British art.

Active to the end Berger returned to Denver unexpectedly early from an art-related trip to England, and he died on June 29, 1999, at the age of seventy-three. He had two memorial services, a traditional Episcopal service at Saint John's Cathedral and a significantly less formal one at the Denver Art Museum, which featured music by Frank Sinatra and Cole Porter, a toast by Denver restaurateur Sam Arnold, and a few choruses of "The Drunken Sailor." He is buried at Fairmount Cemetery.

Rodolfo "Corky" Gonzales speaks to the press in 1979 from the steps of the old West Side Court building, office of Denver District Attorney Dale Tooley who frequently clashed with Gonzales over police and prosecution issues.
COURTESY OF THE *DENVER POST.*

Escuela Tlatelolco, site of the Gonzales Memorial March.

Rodolfo "Corky" Gonzales
1928–2005

The ethnic face of Denver has changed significantly over the past forty years, perhaps most notably by the increase in the Latino population, generally people who are directly or indirectly from Mexico or Central or South America.

The leadership of the Latino community during this time includes Bernard Valdez, who worked in local welfare programs and served on the Denver school board; Lloyd Chavez, owner of Burt's Automotive Group; Paul Sandoval, former state senator and school board member; and Federico Pena, Denver mayor from 1983 to 1991. Yet for many of Latino background, their choice for champion of Latino rights would be someone who was neither elected to office nor achieved great business success: Rodolfo "Corky" Gonzales, perhaps the most outspoken and public figure in what came to be called the "Chicano rights movement."

Gonzales was born in Denver in 1928, the youngest of eight children. His parents were migrant laborers and Mexican nationals. He attended public schools in the state and graduated from Denver's Manual High School in 1944. After high school, Gonzales embarked on a successful bantamweight boxing career, including Golden Gloves championships and the 1947 National Amateur Athletic Union's bantamweight title. He ended his amateur career with a 53–4 record, turned professional in 1948, and went on to compile a 65–9–1 record in his eight years as a pro.

By the 1960s the civil rights movement was in full swing, with marches and demonstrations taking place throughout the country. Although most national attention was on obtaining equal rights for blacks, there was a smaller, parallel effort on behalf of Latinos, and it was to this movement that Gonzales was attracted.

After completing his boxing career, Gonzales, then 28, had gone into the restaurant and bail bond businesses. But he also developed interests in politics and civil rights, and began working with groups seeking better treatment for Latinos and, particularly in Gonzales's case, for those with Mexican backgrounds or—the term he preferred—Chicanos.

Gonzales's popularity as a boxer enabled him to quickly attract a following as a political organizer and a Democratic activist. He became a Democrat district captain, headed the 1960 "Viva Kennedy" campaign to attract Latino voters to the Kennedy ticket in the presidential election, and was appointed by Denver Mayor Tom Currigan to head the Denver Neighborhood Youth Corps. By mid-1966, however, Gonzales had become disillusioned with the Democrats. Kennedy was dead, the country was deeply involved in the Vietnam War—which Gonzales opposed—and he was disappointed by the party's inability to do enough to combat what he saw as pervasive racism and police mistreatment of minorities. He also had a falling out with Currigan, who had fired him from his Youth Corps position.

Gonzales moved quickly to create his own cultural and political organizations, the Crusade for Justice and the La Raza Unida party. He also wrote "I am Joaquin," a poem about a young Chicano addressing issues of ethnic identity. The poem, which was one of the first works in the Chicano literary tradition and became a rallying cry for the Chicano movement, concludes:

We start to MOVE.

La Raza!

Mejicano!

Español!

Latino!

Hispano!

Chicano!

or whatever I call myself,

I look the same

I feel the same

I cry

and

Sing the same

I am the masses of my people and I refuse to be absorbed.

I am Joaquin

The odds are great but my spirit is strong

My faith unbreakable

My blood is pure

I am Aztec Prince and Christian Christ

I SHALL ENDURE!

By 1968 Gonzales, along with Cesar Chavez—who was organizing migrant laborers in the West—began to achieve recognition as a national Latino leader. As the civil rights and anti-Vietnam War movements were reaching their peaks, Gonzales led a Western states group to the Poor Peoples' March on Washington, which had been organized by Martin Luther King, Jr., before his assassination in April 1968, and was led nationally by Jesse Jackson.

In 1970 Gonzales started the Escuela Tlatelolco de Estudios, originally an offshoot of the Crusade for Justice, but which is now a community-based private school in northwest Denver. The school, which combines academics with cultural studies, is run by Gonzales's daughter, Nita.

In 1972 the La Raza Unida party held its only national party convention, but shortly thereafter the party began to dissolve as a result of a leadership dispute between Gonzales and another La Raza Unida faction. The 1970s were difficult for the Crusade for Justice as well. Gonzales's confrontational style of leadership, and his refusal to disavow violence, resulted in continuing conflict with the police and with those in the Latino community who were uncomfortable with Gonzales's brand of activism. Gonzales was jailed briefly in 1971 for carrying a weapon, and two years later a shootout with police occurred near the Crusade for Justice headquarters where, police maintained, explosives were being stored. Gonzales denied the charge.

The controversies kept Gonzales and the Crusade in the spotlight but gradually took their toll on the organization as a new, less-confrontational generation of Latino political leaders emerged and began to assume positions of power in business and government, culminating in Federico Peña's election as mayor in 1983.

In 1987 Gonzales suffered a heart attack, resulting in a car accident and permanent head injuries, which greatly weakened his body as well as his short-term memory. For the last eighteen years of his life, Gonzales lived quietly with his wife, Geraldine, and their large family.

In 2005 his health began to deteriorate rapidly, and he was diagnosed with congestive heart disease. Refusing further treatment, Gonzales checked out of St. Anthony's Hospital in late March and spent the last three weeks of his life at home with family, where he died on April 12, 2005, at the age of seventy-six. His body was cremated.

Even after more than two decades out of the limelight, Gonzales death was national news, including an obituary in the *New York Times* and scores of stories in other national and local publications recalling his career. Today, with Latinos accounting for almost one in every three people in the city of Denver, and almost one in five in metropolitan Denver, it is not difficult to account for their significant political power. Politicians at all levels—from presidential candidates on down—take the Latino vote seriously. Yet such was not the case in the 1960s when Gonzales and his associates began their movement. The Latino population was relatively small, and many Latinos didn't bother to register to vote

The legacy of Gonzales and his followers is similar to that of Malcolm X—whose writings explored many of the same subjects as those of Gonzales—and groups such as the Black Panthers. In both movements there were those like Gonzales and Malcolm X who were concerned about the cultural integrity of their people and were eager, and often impatient, to achieve their goals. As a result, their tactics and rhetoric were often controversial. Yet, without such people would either movement have been as successful? As the *Denver Post* noted in an editorial about Gonzales, "Would Federico Peña have become Denver mayor in 1983 were it not for Corky Gonzales?"

On the Sunday following Gonzales's death a large memorial march was held, going from the Escuela Tlatelolco to Denver's Mestizo-Curtis Park.

Jack Swigert.
COURTESY OF THE NATIONAL AERONAUTICS
AND SPACE ADMINISTRATION.

$\mathscr{J}$OHN LEONARD "JACK" SWIGERT, JR.
1931–1982

"Houston, we've had a problem here."

With those understated words on the evening of April 13, 1970, Jack Swigert notified the NASA control center and the world that the *Apollo 13* mission, which was then orbiting the moon and had been in space for fifty-five hours and fifty-five minutes, was in serious trouble. Just before the lunar landing craft was set to depart for the moon's surface, an oxygen tank in a service module exploded, cutting off the command module's water, electricity, and oxygen. For the next four days the world watched as Denver astronaut Jack Swigert and his fellow crewmen, James Lovell and Fred Haise, along with hundreds of people at NASA's Houston Flight Center, struggled to prevent a major tragedy in space.

Swigert was born on August 30, 1931, in Denver, the son of Virginia and Dr. John Leonard Swigert, Sr., an opthamologist. Swigert grew up at 1746 Kearney Street in Denver's Park Hill neighborhood and, despite being considered small for an interior lineman, starred in football at East High School and the University of Colorado (CU), where he started in thirty consecutive games. In later years, when he became well-known and was asked about his football career, he characteristically downplayed his success, with comments such as "I was usually on the bottom of the pile." In 1953 he graduated from CU with honors and a degree in mechanical engineering. He joined the Air Force, where he became a pilot—an ambition he had pursued from an early age, when he took private flying lessons at Combs

Aviation near what was then Stapleton Field in east Denver.

He served in the U.S. Air Force in Korea, and after the war became a test pilot for Pratt and Whitney, a manufacturer of airplane engines. He continued his education, receiving a master's degree in aerospace science in 1965, and a year later he was accepted by NASA as an astronaut. In 1970, Swigert was named to be a back-up command pilot for the *Apollo 13* mission. He would be part of the team but not part of the flight-crew unless something unexpected happened to one of the three lead crewmen.

It did. Just one day before the launch, astronaut Tom Mattingly was removed from the mission after it was discovered he had been exposed to German measles and was not immune. NASA doctors checked with Swigert's parents in Denver, who confirmed that he had already had German measles as a child. He was immune and was suddenly responsible for piloting the command module on a mission to the moon the following day. At 2:23 P.M. on Saturday, April 11, 1970, *Apollo 13* lifted off from Kennedy Space Center in Florida.

Three days later, disaster struck. An explosion, probably caused by a short circuit, ruptured the oxygen tank in the command ship's service module and the module's cover was blown off. Not only was all the oxygen lost, but the damage also took out the water, electric, and propulsion systems. *Odyssey,* the command module spacecraft that was to return the crew to earth, was crippled and dark. The moon-landing by Lovell and Haise in the lunar-landing vehicle, named *Aquarius,* would obviously have to be cancelled. In fact, the lunar-landing vehicle, which was only designed to support two passengers, was their only hope for a return to earth. Somehow it would have to carry three passengers all the way back from the moon to Earth's orbit, where the crew would return to the stricken command module and try to use emergency battery power for reentry to earth. Only the command module had the kind of shield that could survive the heat of traveling through the earth's atmosphere.

However, there was a major problem. A quick check of positions disclosed that the spacecraft was on a trajectory that, if unchanged, would miss the Earth. A correction was needed to re-aim the spacecraft so the module would hit an ocean on Earth rather than shoot past and continue, forever, into space. The only way to change the trajectory would be to employ an emergency procedure using only the thrusting engine of *Aquarius*. At 3:42 A.M., just five and one-half hours after the explosion, mission control gave the signal to fire the thruster.

The trajectory was reoriented, and the spacecraft appeared to be headed to Earth. For the next four days the world watched and listened as the crew labored successfully in near-freezing and dark conditions to conserve fuel, oxygen, and electricity, and repair the over-taxed carbon dioxide removal system that prevented them from being poisoned.

Cold War animosities gave way to cooperation, as the Soviet government offered to help recover the module if it landed too far away from United States ships. Then, suddenly and unexpectedly, disaster loomed again. After the spacecraft reemerged from its first and only orbit around the moon, still more than 200,000 miles from Earth, the trajectory issue was examined again by NASA's Mission Control, and it became clear that the original calculations had been wrong. The spacecraft still would miss Earth by almost 100 miles. The only solution was another "burn" with the thrusting engine on *Aquarius,* this time attempting a larger mid-course correction that had ever been attempted on an Apollo mission, and using a manual procedure that had never been tried before. But, this time the correction worked perfectly, and the ship headed home.

As the spacecraft neared Earth, the crew climbed from *Aquarius* into the command module, jettisoned *Aquarius,* and entered the Earth's atmosphere at a speed of almost 24,000 miles per hour. The descent went perfectly, and almost six days after launch the module, with parachutes trailing behind, dropped into the Pacific just four miles from the U.S. Navy carrier *Iwo Jima.*

For his service aboard *Apollo 13,* Swigert was awarded the Presidential Medal for Freedom and the NASA Distinguished Service Medal. The mission was featured in the successful 1995 Ron Howard movie *Apollo 13,* in which Kevin Bacon played Swigert. The movie was nominated for five Academy Awards.

Swigert left NASA in 1973 and became executive director of the committee on science and technology for the U.S. House of Representatives. In 1978 he ran unsuccessfully for the United States Senate from Colorado, being defeated by Bill Armstrong in the Republican primary. Armstrong went on to win the general election and Swigert then moved into the private sector, first working with a technology firm engaged in energy and space research, and then for a mining company. The political bug had bitten, however, and Swigert remained interested in running for office. In 1982 he ran for the new sixth congressional seat Colorado had gained as a result of the 1980 census. This time he was easily elected and, at the age of fifty-one, he appeared ready to begin what many expected would be a prominent political career.

It was not to be. For the second time in his life, unexpected circumstances intervened. Swigert became ill early in 1982, and in April underwent surgery to remove what was believed to be a localized cancerous tumor. By September, however, the cancer had spread to his bone marrow and lungs. Echoing the phrase that *Apollo 13* had a "slight problem," Swigert, low-key as always, told reporters that when he heard the news he was "slightly disappointed." Although doctors believed it was still treatable, and Swigert kept up his campaign schedule while receiving medication, he continued to weaken. On December 27, 1982, just one week before he would have been sworn in as the state's newest member of Congress, he died of respiratory failure brought on by the disease. At his side at Georgetown University Hospital in Washington was Bill Armstrong, the man who had defeated Swigert in his first campaign.

Shortly before his death, Swigert had an opportunity to reflect on a life of considerable accomplishments. "I believe God measures your life. He puts you on Earth, gives you talents and certain opportunities and, I think, you're going to be called to account for those opportunities. I don't know how I'll be measured," he said, "but no, I can't think of any opportunities I haven't taken."

Swigert was buried at Mount Olivet Cemetery in a large ceremony attended by political leaders and friends, including his fellow *Apollo 13* astronauts Fred Haise and James Lovell. Lovell gave the eulogy for the man with whom he had shared the damaged spacecraft twelve years earlier and ended his remarks with the words: "The mission is now completed."

John L. "Jack" Swigert's grave at Mount Olivet Cemetery.

Jerry Gart, flanked by his brother Mickey and his uncle Melvin, who were part of a business that was always a family effort.
COURTESY OF SALLY GART AND THE GART FAMILY.

Jerry Gart's gravesite in the Emanuel section of Fairmount Cemetery.

$\mathcal{J}$ERRY GART
1933–1996

In Colorado and many other states, the name
Gart has been linked inextricably to the word "sports." This is due
primarily to one man: Jerry Gart.

Jerry Gart was born in Denver on New Year's Eve in 1933, went
to North High School, and attended the University of Colorado. A
good athlete, he met his wife, Sally, at Winter Park one day when he
was skiing and had stopped to help her after a fall. After their marriage in 1954, Gart joined the small family sporting goods business
that his father, Nathan, had started in 1928 in a 12-by-17-foot storefront space at 1643 Larimer Street.

Gart had a flair for the business, and by 1986 he and his family
had grown the company to seventeen stores and more than 1,000
employees. Along the way he introduced Denver to the term
"Sniagrab" as the name for Gart Sports' enormously successful annual post-Labor Day ski sale. "Sniagrab" ("bargains" spelled backwards)
was originally created—reportedly over a couple of drinks after
work—as a way of quickly selling the previous season's merchandise. But the promotion, which continues to this day under new
ownership, was so successful that in some years Gart Sports reportedly sold more than $20 million worth of merchandise during the
single three-day event.

Certainly the boldest Gart innovation, and ultimately the crown
jewel of the Gart Sports empire, was the huge, seven-story "Sports
Castle" at Tenth Street and Broadway in Denver. The property had

been a Chrysler dealership and had car ramps running from floor to floor. The size of the building, and the odd layout created by the ramps, caused Jerry Gart's father and several other family members to oppose the purchase. But by that time, 1971, Jerry Gart was firmly in control of the business, and the purchase was made. At one time the new Gart Sports headquarters had tennis and basketball courts on the roof and featured indoor golf and skiing practice facilities. It was one of the first category-specific superstores in the country, long before PetSmart or Home Depot. And the car ramps were put to good use: Gart bought a fleet of converted golf carts to carry people and goods throughout the store.

In 1986 the Gart family sold their interest in the stores to Thrifty Corporation of Los Angeles, although Jerry Gart and other family members, including his uncle Melvin and his younger brother Mickey, continued to manage the business for six more years. They expanded into Utah and Missouri, and in 1988 bought out their long-time Colorado-based rival, Dave Cook Sporting Goods. In the early days the rivalry between the Gart and Cook families included more than one fistfight, as the two merchants competed for the same customers in lower downtown Denver.

The success of Gart Sports provided Jerry Gart with time to pursue other interests. He was chairman of the Denver Convention and Visitors Bureau, and served on the boards of Rose Medical Center, the Denver Chamber of Commerce, the Bonfils Foundation, and the Denver Center for the Performing Arts. In 1976 he took up flying, eventually piloting friends and family around the country in his own two-plane fleet, including a Cessna Citation 2 jet. In addition, his work in the sporting goods business went beyond management and marketing skills. He had ample opportunity to try out the products personally, and was an active golfer, skier, hunter, and fisherman.

In 1992 the Gart family ended their association with the stores that still bear their name and concentrated on the real estate business, developing condominiums at Avon, Colorado, near Vail, where Jerry Gart had bought a large house in 1979. Meanwhile, Thrifty sold Gart Sports to Leonard Green and Partners, although the stores continued to be operated under the Gart name. In 1990, shortly after the family had left the Gart Sports business, Jerry Gart suffered the first of several strokes that would weaken him and result in his death in 1996 at the age of sixty-two. He is buried in the Emanuel section of Fairmount Cemetery.

In 1998 Gart Sports went public, and by 2003 the business that began with a tiny storefront on Larimer Street had annual sales of almost one billion dollars, operating stores in twenty-five states under both the original Gart name and the names of the competitors it had acquired: Oshmans and SportMart. In 2003 Gart Sports merged with a larger company, The Sports Authority, which operated 198 stores in 32 states. The resulting entity is the nation's largest sporting goods retailer. The new company, headed by Doug Morton and Marty Hanaka, is still based in Colorado and operates 385 stores in 45 states and in Japan.

While Jerry Gart's children—Ken, Tom, and John—have continued to build their real estate businesses, they have also kept the association between the Gart family and sports alive through a company that owns stores such as Colorado Ski & Golf and local retailers in many major ski areas. Knowing a good idea when they saw one, they adapted their father's idea for a major fall promotion, which now lives on at Colorado Ski & Golf as the "Ski Rex" sale and now competes with "Sniagrab" at Gart Sports.

Alan Berg in his early thirties and before brain surgery forced him to adopt the "Prince Valiant" haircut that characterized his later years.
COURTESY OF JUDITH LEE BERG.

Berg's gravesite at Freesons Waldheim Cemetery in Chicago.
COURTESY OF JULIA TALBOT.

$\mathscr{A}$LAN HARRISON BERG
1934–1984

"Hopefully my legal training will prevent me from saying the one thing that will kill me."

It didn't. Alan Berg's career in the 1970s and 1980s as one of the country's most successful and controversial talk show hosts—"the man you love to hate"—ended in a hail of bullets outside his east Denver condominium on a Monday evening in 1984.

The fifty-year-old Berg's death came at a time when he had developed a national reputation. He was one of the radio personalities featured on the CBS television program *60 Minutes* six months earlier, and he was scheduled to cover that summer's national political conventions for Denver's KOA radio station, where he hosted his highly rated talk show.

Berg's life began in Chicago in 1934, the second child of a dentist, Joseph Berg, and his wife, Ruth. His childhood was spent in comfortable circumstances in Chicago's Hyde Park neighborhood. In 1951 the tall, thin, red-haired Berg decided to go West for college. He enrolled at the University of Colorado, attracted by the skiing, the climate, and the fact that the university had a reputation in Chicago as having a good Jewish fraternity, which Berg joined.

As was the case with many college students in the 1950s, Berg developed an interest in jazz. Also, according to Stephen Singular in his book *Talked to Death,* Berg latched on to the decade's legendary "growing up" novel, J. D. Salinger's *Catcher in the Rye*. The novel's protagonist, Holden Caulfield, spent a good portion of the book berating people he saw as "phonies," a characterization that resonated immediately with Berg, who would spend the rest of his life attacking those he judged to be frauds and hypocrites.

Berg was an intense and restless individual—both physically and intellectually. In addition to the University of Colorado, he attended four other colleges before finally ending his formal education with a law degree from DePaul University in Chicago in 1957. When he passed the Illinois bar examination at the age of twenty-two, he became one of the youngest people ever to do so.

In 1958 Berg married Judith Lee Halpern, daughter of a prominent Denver family, who he had met while attending the University of Colorado. He also began his law practice in Chicago and soon became a highly successful criminal trial lawyer. On the side, he continued his love for jazz, and he and Judith began promoting jazz concerts in Chicago.

Conducting a busy trial practice in criminal law can be a demanding and draining profession. It proved to be particularly difficult for Berg, whose personal moral code began to rebel against some of the people he was defending, reportedly including organized crime figures. Perhaps he asked himself if he was just another of those hypocrites he loathed and if his high-profile, high-spending lifestyle was being built on the backs of innocent victims. Adding to his personal difficulties, Berg suffered from epilepsy and from periodic bouts of depression, which began to threaten his career.

After ten years in Chicago, both Berg's personal life and his career were in trouble. He had become disillusioned with practicing law, was frequently turning to alcohol to try to alleviate his depression, and his marriage was showing signs of strain. In desperation, Judith Berg suggested they move to Denver to try to start over.

Free from the pressures of his fast-paced lifestyle in Chicago, the depression and drinking faded. But his career choices posed a dilemma. Despite his talents as a trial lawyer, he was determined not to resume that life. He turned instead to one of the things that he loved the most: clothes and fashion. He took jobs selling shoes and working in a clothing store, and while he was learning the business he began planning to open his own high-end custom-clothing business. The result was The Shirt Broker, Berg's successful custom clothing shops in downtown Denver and Cherry Creek. It was there that Berg met the man who would change his life. Laurence Gross hosted a talk-radio show on a small, struggling, suburban AM radio station, KWBZ. One day, he suggested that Berg—who was nothing if not talkative—come on his show as a guest. Berg agreed, and the results were notable. Whenever Berg was a guest, the calls increased; and when Gross eventually moved to California, Berg was hired to replace him. Berg's bright, slightly manic, but always direct personality worked very well in the emerging medium of talk-radio.

But no sooner had Berg discovered radio than again his life and his career underwent some changes. First, the radio station came under new management, which urged him to be more controversial. Second, Berg's marriage was again in trouble. By 1976 Judith had moved to Chicago to accept a new job, and it was while visiting her there that Berg suffered what seemed at first to be another epileptic seizure. In fact, it was a brain tumor, and he underwent a long and serious operation that nearly killed him.

When he returned to the microphone, Berg seemed to be a different performer—much more aggressive than he had ever been before—and eager to tackle topics that were controversial and on the edge. Insulting and hanging up on callers became a mainstay of the show. Berg's targets spanned the political and ideological spectrum, although he had a special antipathy toward the religious right-wing. Ratings soared. Long before Rush Limbaugh and the scores of talkers now on radio and cable television stations, Berg was instrumental in helping to create the topical, opinionated talk-radio format, similar in some ways to the iconoclastic stand-up comedy style of Mort Sahl. Before long, it was not just a matter of Berg talking about people and issues, but people talking about Berg. Like his contemporary Hunter

Thompson, Berg created a character and a public personality that, for better or worse, defined him in the eyes of the world.

In 1977 Berg and his wife were divorced, although they would continue to see one another right up to the evening of his death. In 1978 another change in station ownership brought in a management team that was uncomfortable with Berg's style. He was fired, and promptly signed on at KHOW, then one of Denver's more successful AM stations. After being offered more money he returned to KWBZ a year later and in November 1979, Berg, who had begun receiving hate mail and threats, was confronted in the studio by a local Ku Klux Klan leader. Berg claimed he was physically threatened, but criminal charges were not filed. The show continued to do well on KWBZ, and finally in 1981 Berg got an opportunity to make a major career advance, moving up to Denver's top-rated 50,000-watt KOA. His new station, with a signal that covered most of the western United States, brought Berg a wider audience than ever before.

Berg's career at KOA radio continued to be both successful and controversial. He was suspended as a result of a 1982 show when, referring to a woman who claimed she had been choked by Nancy Kissinger, wife of former Secretary of State Henry Kissinger, Berg commented that he wished Mrs. Kissinger had succeeded.

When Berg returned, many felt he began to change his style. He seemed to be more relaxed and less given to the outbursts that had characterized his show before. Many who knew Berg said the changes were real, reflecting his good relationship with a woman and that he had begun to feel confident and secure about his broadcasting career. As with many performers, pushing the limits had gotten him to the top, but once there he increasingly felt more comfortable just being himself: still very outspoken, but not as edgy or gratuitously rude as before.

By June of 1984 Berg's professional and private lives were both doing well. He had been featured on the CBS Television's *60 Minutes* show about talk radio and was getting ready to cover that summer's national political conventions. It seemed possible that he would soon be in a position to develop a show for a national audience.

Unfortunately, he had also come to the attention of "The Order," a small group of neo-Nazis based, for the most part, in the northwest United States, where KOA's strong signal sometimes reached. Infuriated by Berg's frequent attacks and the ridicule he directed at white supremacist organizations, they targeted him for revenge.

At about 9:00 P.M. on the evening of June 18, after having dinner with his former wife, Berg was shot to death as he left his car to enter his condominium at 1445 Adams Street in Denver. There was little evidence and there were no solid leads. Because of his notoriety, the murder of Berg commanded national headlines and resulted in massive police activity for several weeks—but the investigation appeared to be going nowhere.

The case was not broken until a previously unrelated FBI investigation turned up evidence pointing to the neo-Nazi group. Some members of that group, facing prosecution for a variety of other crimes, provided the FBI with important evidence against those they said had plotted Berg's killing.

For a variety of technical evidentiary reasons, the case against the suspects was never prosecuted under Colorado law as a murder. Instead, eleven members of the group were brought to trial in Seattle in September 1985 on a long list of federal charges, including violating Berg's civil rights. Those believed to have been most directly involved in the shooting of Berg were found guilty of several charges and sentenced to prison terms of up to one hundred years.

Berg was buried at the Freesons Waldheim Cemetery in Forest Park, Chicago. On his tombstone are the words "Run Bambi, Run," the warning shout of the mother deer in the 1942 Disney movie *Bambi*. The Bambi quotation on the tombstone was included at the request of Berg's sister and mother, who gave him the nickname "Bambi" when he was a skinny, gangling, slightly awkward youth, like the fawn in the movie. In the movie, Bambi made it to safety.

Hunter S. Thompson in his favorite working space in his Woody Creek home in 1997.
PHOTO BY HELEN DAVIS. COURTESY OF THE *DENVER POST.*

Owl Farm in Woody Creek, Colorado. This was Thompson's home for thirty-eight years. His ashes were dispersed in the air above the farm, shot from a cannon.

*H*UNTER STOCKTON THOMPSON
1937–2005

The 1970s saw the transformation of Aspen, Colorado, from a popular former mining town with several good ski areas into a trendy resort that is home to scores of movie stars, business tycoons, and trust-fund beneficiaries, as well as their private jets. The dirt roads, mom-and-pop stores, and A-frame houses have given way to a community characterized by fur coats and high-end retailers and where the average home price is several million dollars. It is one of the strange ironies of Aspen's history that two of the people who helped put Aspen at the top of the celebrity map in the 1970s were singer John Denver and journalist Hunter Thompson. Denver and Thompson lived near Aspen and, reportedly, intensely disliked one another.

Although each struggled with his fame, and with substance abuse, one could hardly imagine two more opposite public personalities than the upbeat and wholesome Denver, and the dark, angry, even menacing, Thompson, who once was quoted as saying, "I hate to advocate drugs, alcohol, violence or insanity to anyone, but they've always worked for me."

Thompson was born in Louisville, Kentucky, on July 18, 1937, and was the son of an insurance agent. He was educated in Louisville public schools, where his talents as a writer were recognized by a high school English teacher. He also became a fairly active juvenile delinquent, and in 1956 when he was nineteen, he was brought before a Kentucky court and, as sometimes happened with young men with no prior serious record, he was given the option of going to jail or entering the military. He chose the Air Force, and began writing for the *Command Courier,* the newspaper at Eglin Air Force Base in northwest Florida. Despite his lack of any formal journalism training Thompson—who loved sports—worked his way up to sports editor. He received an honorable discharge as an airman second class in 1958, although not without annoying his superiors, one of whom noted his rebellious attitude and wrote that Thompson, "although talented, will not be guided by policy."

For the next few years Thompson continued to pursue journalism as a career in a variety of jobs, including working as a foreign correspondent and writing for various magazines and newspapers. He married his first wife, Sandy, in 1963, and the couple's son, Juan, was born in 1964. The family moved to the still relatively unspoiled town of Aspen in 1967, the same year the Snowmass Ski Area opened, and just three years after the streets of Aspen were paved.

Thompson burst onto the national literary scene in late 1966 with the publication of *Hell's Angels,* a firsthand account of several months he spent with the motorcycle gang. This was followed in 1971 with the extremely successful *Fear and Loathing in Las Vegas,* a fictionalized account of a wild, drug-enhanced trip to that city by Thompson (in the guise of his alter-ego Raoul Duke), which was made into a 1998 movie starring Johnny Depp. His third book, *Fear and Loathing: On the Campaign Trail,* was published in 1973 and contains Thompson's unique and highly personal coverage of the 1972 presidential campaign from the vantage point of his job as a journalist for *Rolling Stone* magazine. The book gave Thompson an opportunity to vilify his favorite target, Richard Nixon, although many other politicians also were subjected to the Thompson treatment.

This trilogy established his reputation as an innovative and exciting journalist, the creator of something that came to be called "gonzo journalism." The term describes a personal and impressionistic style, in which the writer becomes a major part of the narrative, and facts blend with fiction in the interest of creating a strong and bold account of events. In creating his form of writing, Thompson was influenced by many writers, including Ernest Hemingway, H. L. Mencken, F. Scott Fitzgerald and, perhaps most of all, Jack Kerouac. Kerouac's 1957 *On The Road,* became a kind of Bible for what came to be called the Beat Generation, an iconoclastic social and literary movement which influenced Thompson. There are many parallels between Kerouac's highly personalized account of his hedonistic drug- and alcohol-influenced travels across the country and Thompson's books, particularly *Fear and Loathing in Las Vegas.*

However, while Kerouac's book earned him cult status, Thompson's trilogy earned him that plus considerable wealth and fame. All three of his first books were bestsellers, and the former itinerant journalist began to receive lucrative writing offers from prominent publishers.

Like no other writer of his day, Thompson became both the story-teller and the story. His own lifestyle became the subject of articles, books, movies, and even a *Doonesbury* comic strip, where Thompson was the model for Uncle Duke, a gun-loving, substance-abusing mani-ac, who in one strip fired one of his weapons in the direction of an unseen neighbor who was singing "Colorado, Rocky Mountain High." John Denver, of course. Reportedly, Thompson disliked the comic strip and its author, Gary Trudeau, as much as he disliked Denver.

Two subjects that Thompson cared passionately about were sports and politics. Sports came first, and Thompson was even able to temper his strong dislike of Richard Nixon as he came to appre-ciate the thirty-seventh president not as a politician, but as a fan and a student of football. His interest in politics apparently developed after he attended the infamous 1968 Democratic National Convention in Chicago, where he was among those who were injured in skirmishes between protesters and the police.

Returning to Aspen, he launched a bizarre campaign for sheriff of Pitkin County on the "Freak Power" ticket. His platform featured promises that were largely irrelevant and certainly beyond a county sheriff's authority—including legalizing drugs, replacing the streets of Aspen with bike paths, and changing the name of the rapidly gentrifying town to Fat City. But his platform appealed to the "sex, drugs, and rock and roll" crowd that could still afford to hang around Aspen in those days, as well as to many in the valley who feared that the area was being over-developed. Thompson lost the race, but barely. He actually won a plurality in the city of Aspen, and received 44 percent of the vote countywide. He continued to support efforts to limit expensive and high-density building in the valley, and in the wake of his 1970 race, voters in both Aspen and Pitkin County elected many no-growth or slow-growth candidates, who stemmed some of the tidal wave of development, for a time. Although Thompson railed against politics and politicians, he never lost his faith in the political process itself and was an active member of the Woody Creek Caucus, one of the more effective community action groups in Pitkin County.

He also continued to write, and at the time of his death he had published a total of fifteen books including a novel and two books of his voluminous and entertaining private correspondence—revealing, among other things, a "kinder, gentler," and more vulnerable side of Thompson, which may come as a surprise to those who did not know him. His last book, published in 2004, was *Hey Rube: Blood Sport, the Bush Doctrine, and the Downward Spiral of Dumbness*. Although there is general agreement among critics that his best books were his first three, it indicates something about his considerable talent that at the time of his death almost all of his books were still in print and continued to attract a large and loyal following.

In 1980 Thompson and his first wife were divorced, and in 2003 he married his second wife, Anita, who had long been his assistant.

During the 1980s and 1990s Thompson, in addition to turning

out his books and following the lecture circuit, worked at various times as a critic and correspondent for several publications, including *Rolling Stone* and the *San Francisco Examiner.*

His life at his self-described "fortified compound" at Owl Farm in Woody Creek, just west of Aspen, continued to be well documented, as did his lifestyle: raising exotic peacocks, enjoying a variety of legal and illegal substances, entertaining friends who came to visit, including many celebrities, and collecting and shooting firearms. A particular Thompson favorite was said to be "shotgun golf," a kind of pitch-and-putt game with the added feature that under certain circumstances players could try to destroy an opponent's golf ball with shots from their sidearms. Such antics amused many of Thompson's friends and fans, who seemed to celebrate his lifestyle. But there was another side to it all: the sad side of an aging and infirm cult figure trapped in the bizarre and ultimately unsustainable identity he had created thirty years before, someone still deeply addicted to drugs. In the words of Rich Cohen, a sympathetic *Rolling Stone* editor and one of the last people to interview Thompson before his death, he "never figured out how to grow old."

The timing, if not the manner, of Thompson's death came as a surprise to his friends and family. Although he had been in poor health for some time, and had recently had spinal and hip replacement surgeries, he gave no clue of his intention to take his own life on the afternoon of Sunday, February 24, 2005. Sitting in his favorite chair in his kitchen, in front of his favorite typewriter, with a glass of his favorite beverage, Chivas Regal, Thompson ended his life with a single gunshot from a .45 handgun. His son, daughter-in-law, and grandson were in the house, although not in the room, and his wife was in Aspen at a health club. Upon discovering what Thompson had done, his family—soon to be joined by close friends—voiced support for his decision to end life on his own terms.

Two weeks following his death and cremation, a memorial service of sorts was held at the Jerome Hotel in Aspen, home of the Jerome Bar, a frequent Thompson haunt. Among the more than 200 attending and exchanging Thompson stories and memories were actors Jack Nicholson, Johnny Depp, Sean Penn, and Bill Murray, *Rolling Stone* publisher Jann Wenner, both of Thompson's wives, his son, and his brother.

Thompson's official finale, however, was as unique and bizarre as his life had been. On the evening of August 20, 2005, and at his request, his ashes—along with a variety of fireworks—were shot several hundred feet into the sky over his Owl Creek Farm home in a $2.5-million ceremony attended by hundreds of friends and fans, as well as international media representatives. Among those participating were several Hollywood stars and John Kerry and George McGovern, former Democratic candidates for the presidency. Following the spectacular event, Thompson's longtime illustrator, Ralph Steadman, who knew Thompson better than most, told the *Denver Post* he suspected Thompson's own reaction to the day's events would have been that "it wasn't quite big enough."

$\mathcal{J}$OHN DENVER
1943–1997

On the morning of October 13, 1997, headlines throughout the world announced the death in a small, private airplane crash of the man who was perhaps Colorado's most well-known celebrity, fifty-three-year-old singer and songwriter John Denver.

Late the previous afternoon, Denver, who lived in Aspen, Colorado, had been piloting a small custom-built, experimental single-engine plane that ran out of fuel and plunged into the Pacific Ocean near Monterey, California.

Denver was born in Roswell, New Mexico, on December 31, 1943. His name was John Henry Deutschendorf, and his father, who was in the Air Force, was stationed at a base nearby. His father's career caused the family to move frequently while Denver was growing up and also launched him into the life-long love affair with planes and aviation that would eventually kill him.

By the time Denver entered Texas Tech University to study architecture, he had also begun playing the guitar and singing at local folk music clubs. In 1964, at the age of twenty-one, he dropped out of college and moved to Los Angeles. Aiming for a career in show business, he decided his last name was a liability, and changed it from Deutschendorf to Denver, based on the fact that it sounded right to him and that—still several years before living there—he had developed a liking for Colorado and the Rocky Mountains.

He managed to find work right away, and in 1965 replaced Chad Mitchell in the popular folk group The Chad Mitchell Trio. After four

John Denver.
COURTESY OF THE COLORADO HISTORICAL SOCIETY.

One of the engraved stones in the John Denver Sanctuary in Aspen.

years touring with the group, renamed the Mitchell Trio, he quit and began performing on his own, often singing songs he had written. He also met and married Annie Martell in 1967.

Success came quickly. By 1971 his song "Take Me Home Country Road" was a hit, followed in 1972 by "Rocky Mountain High," which was written about Aspen. He and Annie had moved to Aspen in 1970 and built a house in what was then a relatively undeveloped area called Starwood, just west of Aspen. In 1969 his parents had retired and moved to Denver. For the next ten years, Denver's musical career was characterized by one hit song after another. Several of his single records and albums reached the number one spot in sales, and his *Greatest Hits* album sold more than ten million copies. He was named Country Music Entertainer of the Year in 1975. He also wrote songs for others, including "Leaving on a Jet Plane," which was the biggest hit for the group Peter, Paul, and Mary.

Denver was also able to translate his success as a singer into television and movies. He made many television shows and specials, won an Emmy for television in 1975, and co-starred with George Burns in the hit 1977 film *Oh God!* in which he showed a talent for comedic acting.

He also became associated with several causes, including issues related to the environment, hunger, and the peace movement. In 1976 he started the Windstar Foundation as a nonprofit environmental research and education project, and he served as a member of a presidential commission on world and domestic hunger.

Although most of the public liked them, Denver's songs and his message were not universally beloved. Some critics felt his lyrics were too shallow, sugary, and optimistic, and many in Aspen had mixed feelings about the publicity that Denver attracted and the effect it had on their hopes to keep the community relatively unspoiled and livable. Denver's differences with the Aspen community were not helped when he made the mistake of installing two 2,000-gallon gas tanks at his home at the height of the severe 1979 gas shortages. His image as an environmentalist was tarnished, and he was forced to remove the tanks the following year.

By the 1980s Denver's life began to hit some rough spots. His wife, Annie, was granted a divorce in 1982, and as the decade wore on his popularity as a performer began to wane and his record company, RCA, eventually dropped him.

The last decade of his life was marked by more ups and downs. In 1988 he married Cassandra Delaney, an Australian actress, but three years later they were divorced. In 1989 he joined the Nitty Gritty Dirt Band to record an album that was named album of the year by the Country Music Association, and in 1994 he published *Take Me Home: An Autobiography*. His 1995 Wildlife Concert, to benefit the Wildlife Conservation Society, was well received on television and issued as a video. He also was arrested twice for drunken driving, in 1993 and 1994. He pleaded guilty to a reduced charge in the first case and was awaiting trial in the second case when he died.

By the time of his death, Denver's relationship with his former wives appeared to be improving and he was receiving treatment for an alcohol problem. Although there had been speculation that the airplane crash may have been caused by alcohol or drugs, the autopsy found no evidence of either substance. Instead, it was concluded that the crash was caused by an insufficient amount of fuel in one of the plane's tanks, as well as Denver's unfamiliarity with the controls that were used to switch to the auxiliary tank. Memorial services were held for Denver in both Denver and Aspen, where his ashes were scattered in a private ceremony.

The John Denver Sanctuary near the Roaring Fork River in downtown Aspen contains several large stones that include a memorial marker and lyrics of several of his songs. A dense grove of trees on the east side of Aspen Mountain has been dedicated as the John Denver Memorial Grotto. And although Colorado's official state song is *Where the Columbines Grow* by A. J. Fynn, a little-known song that was selected by the state in 1915, Denver's 1972 *Rocky Mountain High* is—and will likely remain—the unofficial favorite.

$\mathcal{S}$OURCES

The primary sources for this book are the collections of the Colorado Historical Society and the Denver Public Library, notably the newspaper clipping and microfilm collections in the Western History and Genealogy Department at the Denver Public Library. The clipping files containing stories from the *Denver Post, Rocky Mountain News,* and other newspapers throughout the state are an invaluable resource for the researcher. An unexpected bonus was a gift by friend and neighbor Jennifer Hulac. In the interest of clearing out her garage she gave me boxes containing complete sets of back issues of *Colorado Magazine,* published by the Colorado Historical Society. The volumes dated from the 1940s to the 1960s and proved particularly valuable as a source of interesting and often arcane tidbits, which were seemingly unavailable elsewhere.

In addition, many other sources were used, including:

Books:

Ambrose, S. *Citizen Soldiers: The U.S. Army from the Normandy Beaches to the Bulge to the Surrender of Germany.* New York: Simon & Schuster, 1997.

Arps, Louise Ward. *Denver in Slices.* Athens, Ohio: Swallow Press/Ohio University Press, 1959.

Bancroft, Caroline. *Six Racy Madams of Colorado.* Boulder, Colo.: Johnson Publishing Co., 1965.

Bean, Geraldine. *Charles Boettcher: A Study in Pioneer Western Enterprise.* Boulder, Colo.: Westview Press, 1976.

Brettell, R. R. *Historic Denver: The Architects and the Architecture 1858–1893.* Denver: Historic Denver Guides, 1979.

Brown, Kenneth A. *Four Corners: History, Land and People of the Desert Southwest.* New York: HarperCollins, 1995.

Bueler, Gladys R. *Colorado's Colorful Characters.* Boulder, Colo.: Pruett Publishing Co., 1981.

Cable, Mary. *To Cure, To Help, To Comfort: The Life of Dr. James J. Waring.* N.p.: 1996.

Cervi, Clé, *100 Moore Years.* Denver: Moore School PTSA.

Collis, J. *John Denver, Mother Nature's Son.* Edinburgh: Mainstream Publishing Co., 1999.

Cowperthwaite, Jill. *It's a Darn Good Question, Reflections on the life of Dr. Florence Rena Sabin,* a private research study for the Denver Fortnightly Club, 2003.

Decker, Peter R. *The Utes Must Go!* Golden, Colo.: Fulcrum Publishing Co., 2004.

Downing, Sybil, and Robert E. Smith. *Tom Patterson.* Niwot, Colo.: University of Colorado Press, 1995.

Drummond, Alexander. *Enos Mills: Citizen of Nature.* Niwot, Colo.: University of Colorado Press, 1995.

Fay, Abbott. *Famous Coloradans: 124 People Who Have Gained Nationwide Fame.* Paonia, Colo.: Mountaintop Productions, 1990.

Fowler, Gene. *Timberline: A Story of Bonfils and Tammen.* Garden City, N.Y.: Garden City Publishing Co., 1947.

Geiger, Helen M. *The Broadmoor Story.* Denver: Smith-Brooks, 1968.

Goldberg, Robert Alan. *Hooded Empire: The Ku Klux Klan in Colorado.* Champaigne, Ill.: University of Illinois Press, 1981.

Goodstein, Phil. *Exploring Jewish Colorado.* Denver: Rocky Mountain Jewish Historical Society, Center for Judaic Studies, University of Denver, 1992.

Goodstein, Phil. *Denver in Our Time: A People's History of the Modern Mile High City.* Denver: New Social Publications, 1999.

Goodstein, Phil. *DIA and Other Scams.* Denver: New Social Publications, 2000.

Halaas, David Fridtjov. *Fairmount and Historic Colorado.* Denver: Fairmount Cemetery Association, 1976.

Hosokawa, Bill. *Thunder in the Rockies: The Incredible* Denver Post. New York: William Morrow & Co., 1976.

Jessen, Kenneth. *Colorado Gunsmoke.* Loveland, Colo.: JV Publications, 1986.

Johnson, Charles A. *Denver's Mayor Speer.* Denver: Green Mountain Press, 1969.

Kronstadt, Janet. *Florence Sabin.* New York: Chelsea House Publishers 1990.

Lamm, R. D., and D. A. Smith. *Pioneers and Politicians: 10 Colorado Governors in Profile.* Boulder, Colo.: Pruett Publishing Co., 1984.

Miller, Max. *Holladay Street.* New York: Ballantine Books, 1962.

Monnett, John H., and Michael McCarthy. *Colorado Profiles: Men and Women Who Shaped the Centennial State.* Niwot, Colo.: University of Colorado Press, 1986.

Noel, Thomas J., and Stephen J. Leonard. *Denver, Mining Camp to Metropolis.* Niwot, Colo.: University of Colorado Press. 1990.

Noel, Thomas J., and Barbara S. Norgren. *Denver: The City Beautiful and its Architects, 1893–1941.* Denver: Historic Denver, Inc., 1987.

Noel, Thomas J., and Cathleen M. Norman. *A Pike's Peak Partnership: The Penroses and the Tutts.* Boulder, Colo.: University Press of Colorado, 2000.

Noel, Thomas J., Stephen J. Leonard, Kevin E. Rucker. *Colorado Givers: A History of Philanthropic Heroes.* Niwot, Colo.: University of Colorado Press, 1998.

Ossad, Steven L., and Don R. Marsh. *Major General Maurice Rose: WWII's Greatest Forgotten Commander.* Lanham, M.d.: Taylor Trade Publishing, 2003.

Paton, Patricia. *A Medical Gentleman, James J. Waring M.D.* Denver: Colorado Historical Society, 1993.

Riley, J. A. *The Biographical Encyclopedia of the Negro Baseball Leagues.* New York: Carrol & Graf Publishers, 1994.

Rosa, Joseph G., and Robin May. *Buffalo Bill and his Wild West: A Pictorial Biography.* Lawrence, Kan.: University of Kansas Press, 1989.

Secrest, Clark. *Hell's Belles: Denver's Brides of the Multitudes.* Boulder, Colo.: University Press of Colorado, 2002.

Smith, Duane A. *Horace Tabor: His Life and the Legend.* Boulder, Colo.: Colorado Associated University Press, 1973.

Smith, David P., and Cynthia S. Becker. *Chipeta, Queen of the Utes.* Montrose, Colo.: Western Reflections Publishing Co., 2003.

Smith, David P. *Ouray, Chief of the Utes.* Ridgeway, Colo.: Wayfinder Press, 1990.

Sprague, Marshall. *Massacre: The Tragedy at White River.* Lincoln: University of Nebraska Press, 1957.

Steckmesser, Kent Ladd. *The Western Hero in History and Legend.* Norman, Ohio: University of Oklahoma Press, 1965.

Stone, W. F. *History of Colorado.* Chicago: S. J. Clarke Publishing Co., 1918.

Talmadge, Marian, and Iris Gilmore. *Barney Ford, Black Baron.* New York: Dodd, Mead & Co., 1973.

Ubbelohde, Carl, Maxine Benson, and Duane A. Smith. *A Colorado History.* Boulder, Colo.: Pruett Publishing Company, 1995.

Varnell, Jeanne. *Women of Consequence: The Colorado Women's Hall of Fame.* Boulder, Colo.: Johnson Books, 1999.

Wommack, Linda. *From the Grave, A Roadside Guide to Colorado's Pioneer Cemeteries.* Caldwell, Id.: Caxton Press, 1998.

Websites:

Bernard, Bush. "Oliver 'The Ghost' Marcelle." Laforche.com Sports. http://lafourche.com/sports/ghost.htm.

Schulte, Melvin. "Buffalo Bill as Reported in Newspapers." R. J. Brown and the Newspaper Collectors Society of America. http://www.HistoryBuff.com.

Colorado Historical Society. "Historical Guide to Colorado Architects." http://www.coloradohistory-oahp.org/index.html.

Colorado State Archives. "Colorado State Archives Online." http://www.colorado.gov/dpa/doit/archives/.

Ekwall, Steve. "Baby Doe Tabor." Colorado Videos Com. http://babydoetabor.com/.

Colorado ODDities. http://www.diac.com/~ekwall2/info/coloddity.shtml.

Encyclopedia Britannica. "Encyclopedia Britannica Online." http://www.britannica.com/.

Enos Mills Cabin. "Enos Mills Cabin Museum and Gallery." http://home.earthlink.net/~enosmillscbn/.

Escuela Tlatelolco. "Rodolfo Corky Gonzales 1928 – 2005, Obituary." http://escuelatlatelolco.org/corky.html.

Heritage Preservation Services. "GWSAC Battle Summaries: Glorieta Pass." http://www.cr.nps.gov/hps/abpp/battles/nm002.htm.

Highbeam Research Inc. "Encyclopedia.com: Horace Austin Warner Tabor." http://www.encyclopedia.com/html/t/tabor-h1o.asp.

Old Estes. "Notables of Old Estes Park: Enos Mills in Estes Park." http://www.oldestes.com/EnosMills.htm.

Iliff School of Theology. "Iliff School of Theology." http://www.iliff.edu/.

Kanzeg, D. "DoeHeads," http://babydoe.org/index.php.

Kestenbaum, Lawrence. "The Political Graveyard." http://politicalgrave-yard.com/.

Noel, T. "Denver History." http://www.denvergov.org/AboutDenver/history.asp.

Pagewise, Inc. "AllSands Music Biographies: John Denver." http://www.all-sands.com/Music/Bio/johndenver_wtm_gn.htm.

Public Broadcasting Service. "New Perspectives on the West." http://www.pbs.org/weta/thewest/.

Rocky Mountain News. http://www.rockymountainnews.com/.

Rocky Mountain News. "Colorado Millenium 2000." http://www.denver-rmn.com/millennium/1228mile.shtml.

Denver Post. http://www.denverpost.com/.

Personal Interviews:

In addition to the secondary sources mentioned above, personal interviews with several families and associates of people included in the book provided additional information, as well as photographs.

*I*NDEX

Page numbers in italics indicate photographs.

Richard Wood is a Denver lawyer and business-man, and was a reporter for the *Rocky Mountain News*. *Here Lies Colorado* is his first book.

Wood received his undergraduate degree in history at the University of Kansas, a law degree from Georgetown Law Center, and a master's degree in political science from New York University. In addition to practicing law in Denver, he was an executive with BellSouth, in Atlanta, and Westinghouse Broadcasting and Cable, in Los Angeles. A native of Kansas City, he lives in Denver with his wife, Amy, and their two sons, Joe and Max.